Uncertainty and Possibility

Also Available From Bloomsbury

Anthropologies and Futures, edited by Juan Francisco Salazar,
Sarah Pink, Andrew Irving and Johannes Sjöberg
Design Anthropological Futures, edited by Rachel Charlotte Smith, Ton Otto,
Kasper Tang Vangkilde, Joachim Halse, Thomas Binder
and Mette Gislev Kjaersgaard
Design Anthropology, edited by Wendy Gunn, Ton Otto and
Rachel Charlotte Smith
Design as Future-Making, edited by Susan Yelavich
and Barbara Adams
Digital Materialities, edited by Sarah Pink, Elisenda Ardèvol and
Dèbora Lanzeni

Uncertainty and Possibility

New Approaches to Future Making in Design Anthropology

Yoko Akama, Sarah Pink
and Shanti Sumartojo

BLOOMSBURY ACADEMIC
LONDON • NEW YORK • OXFORD • NEW DELHI • SYDNEY

BLOOMSBURY ACADEMIC
Bloomsbury Publishing Plc
50 Bedford Square, London, WC1B 3DP, UK
1385 Broadway, New York, NY 10018, USA

BLOOMSBURY, BLOOMSBURY ACADEMIC and the Diana logo are
trademarks of Bloomsbury Publishing Plc

First published in Great Britain 2018
Reprinted by Bloomsbury Academic 2018

Copyright © Sarah Pink, Yoko Akama, Shanti Sumartojo and Contributors, 2018

Sarah Pink, Yoko Akama and Shanti Sumartojo have asserted their right under the
Copyright, Designs and Patents Act, 1988, to be identified as Editors of this work.

For legal purposes the Acknowledgements on p. viii constitute an
extension of this copyright page.

Cover image © Dion Tuckwell

All rights reserved. No part of this publication may be reproduced or transmitted in any form or
by any means, electronic or mechanical, including photocopying, recording, or any information
storage or retrieval system, without prior permission in writing from the publishers.

Bloomsbury Publishing Plc does not have any control over, or responsibility for,
any third-party websites referred to or in this book. All internet addresses given in
this book were correct at the time of going to press. The author and publisher regret
any inconvenience caused if addresses have changed or sites have ceased to exist,
but can accept no responsibility for any such changes.

A catalogue record for this book is available from the British Library.

Library of Congress Cataloging-in-Publication Data
Names: Pink, Sarah, author. | Akama, Yoko, author. | Sumartojo, Shanti, author.
Title: Uncertainty and possibility : new approaches to future making in
design anthropology / Sarah Pink, Yoko Akama, and Shanti Sumartojo.
Description: 1st edition. | New York, NY : Bloomsbury Academic, an imprint of
Bloomsbury Publishing Plc, 2018. | Includes bibliographical references and
index.
Identifiers: LCCN 2017046921| ISBN 9781350002708 (hardcover) | ISBN
1350002704 (hardcover) | ISBN 9781350002715 (paperback) | ISBN 1350002712
(paperback) | ISBN 9781350002685 (ePDF) | ISBN 1350002682 (ePDF) | ISBN
9781350002692 (ePUB) | ISBN 1350002690 (ePUB)
Subjects: LCSH: Design–Anthropological aspects. | Maker movement. |
Architectural design. | Uncertainty.
Classification: LCC NK1520 .P56 2018 | DDC 729–dc23
LC record available at https://lccn.loc.gov/2017046921

ISBN: PB: 978-1-3500-0271-5
HB: 978-1-3500-0270-8
ePDF: 978-1-3500-0268-5
eBook: 978-1-3500-0269-2

Series: Bloomsbury Ethics, 1234567X, volume 6

Typeset by Deanta Global Publishing Services, Chennai, India
Printed and bound in Great Britain

To find out more about our authors and books visit
www.bloomsbury.com and sign up for our newsletters.

Contents

List of Figures		vi
Acknowledgements		viii
Author Biographies		ix
1	Approaching Uncertainty	1
2	What is Uncertainty?	19
3	Uncertainty as Technology	39
4	Strategies for Disruption *Yoko Akama, Sarah Pink, Dèbora Lanzeni, Elisenda Ardèvol, Katherine Moline, Ann Light and Shanti Sumartojo*	59
5	Surrendering to and Tracing Uncertainty *Tom Jackson, Yoko Akama, Sarah Pink and Shanti Sumartojo*	81
6	Uncertainty as Technology for Moving Beyond *David Carlin, Yoko Akama, Sarah Pink and Shanti Sumartojo*	103
7	Propositions and Practical Applications	125
References		133
Index		142

List of Figures

1.1	A *Design+Ethnography+Futures* workshop commencing	1
1.2	A collaborative practice as cat's cradle	4
1.3	Video and photography	9
1.4	Design documentations from *Mindfulness and Technology* workshop	14
2.1	Hard hats – and obsession with risk	19
2.2	Participants improvising in *Spaces of Innovation* workshop (see colour plate section)	
3.1	Material-making using playful practices with yarn and wires	39
3.2	Uncertainty postcards	41
3.3	The *FabPod*: an acoustically designed meeting space as a technology (see colour plate section)	
3.4	Video documentation in *Myths of the Near Future* (see colour plate section)	
4.1	The hungry digital ghost	59
4.2	A sterile space transformed (see colour plate section)	
4.3	Lunch-making and observing (see colour plate section)	
4.4	The brown and orange group making (see colour plate section)	
4.5	An observer, Ann Light, tasting (see colour plate section)	
5.1	The entrance to the undercroft	81
5.2	A building with many myths and a mysterious aura	84
5.3	Simon Bowen's photo that traces Scott McLaughlin's movement across the room (see colour plate section)	
5.4	'A breadcrumb trail is a way to explore space, so we just touch' (see colour plate section)	
5.5	Two-acre space for acoustic exploration (see colour plate section)	
6.1	A parody of certainty	103

6.2	Peering inside one of the portholes of the *FabPod* during the workshop (see colour plate section)	
6.3	Participants writing in the corridor outside the *FabPod* space (see colour plate section)	
7.1	A movement of light	125

Acknowledgements

We thank all the guest facilitators and participants who took part in the *Design+Ethnography+Futures* workshop series, and without whom our work and this book would not have been possible. Our thanks also goes to Dion Tuckwell who designed the image of the book cover as well as many *Design+Ethnography+Futures* digital publications. We would also like to thank Anna Farago, Sarah Kushinsky, Nico Leonard and Annie Fergusson for their amazing organization and assistance in several workshops. This work would not have been possible without the generous support from Design Futures Lab research group, non-fiction lab research group, Digital Ethnography Research Centre, the School of Media and Communication, and former Design Research Institute at RMIT University.

Author Biographies

Yoko Akama is a design researcher in the School of Design and co-leads the *Design+Ethnography+Futures* research programme with Prof. Sarah Pink at RMIT University, Australia. She also established the Design and Social Innovation in Asia-Pacific network (http://desiap.org/). Her Japanese heritage has embedded a Zen-informed reflexive practice to carve a 'tao' (path) in human-centred design. Her practice is entangled in complex 'wicked problems', shaped by working with regional communities in Australia in strengthening their resilience for disaster preparedness and with Indigenous Nations enact their sovereignty and self-determination. She is Adjunct Fellow of an ecosystem innovation studio, Re:public Japan and Visiting Fellow at the Centre of Excellence in Media Practice, Bournemouth University. She is a recipient of several major research grants in Australia and the UK and winner of the prestigious Good Design Australia Awards (2014).

Elisenda Ardévol is Associate Professor in Social Anthropology at the Department of Arts and Humanities, at the Universitat Oberta de Catalunya and director of mediaccions Digital Culture Research Group in Barcelona. She participates in different international Master and Phd programs in media, digital and visual anthropology and has been Visiting Scholar at the Visual Anthropology Centre of the University of Southern California, Los Angeles and EU Centre Visiting Fellow at the Digital Ethnography Centre, RMIT, Melbourne. Her main research lines are related with digital culture, visuality and media in everyday life. Currently, she is exploring design, creativity and collaborative practices in digital technologies. Her publications include 'Digital ethnography and media practices' in Darling-Wolf, *Research Methods in Media Studies* (2014); 'Virtual/Visual Ethnography: Methodological Crossroads at the Intersection of Visual and Internet Research' in Pink, *Advances in Visual Methodology* (2012); 'Playful Media Practices: Theorising New Media Cultural Production' in Brauchler and Postill, *Theorising Media and Practice* (2010);

she is also the editor of *Researching Media through Practices* (2009) and has authored the following books (in Spanish): *Key Debates* (2014), *A Gaze's Quest* (2006) and *Representation and Audiovisual Culture in Contemporary Societies* (2004).

David Carlin is an associate professor, co-founder of the non/fictionLab and co-director of WrICE at RMIT University, Melbourne. Author of two books of creative non-fiction, *The Abyssinian Contortionist* (UWAP, 2015) and *Our Father Who Wasn't There* (Scribe, 2010), he also co-edited *The Near and the Far* (with Francesca Rendle-Short, 2016) and *Performing Digital* (with Laurene Vaughan, Routledge, 2015). In 2016, his radio feature/essay with Kyla Brettle, *Making Up: 11 Scenes from a Bangkok Hotel*, won four Gold and Silver awards at the New York Festivals Awards. David's essays have appeared in *Griffith Review*, *Essay Daily*, *Overland*, *TEXT Journal*, *New Writing*, *Media International Australia*, *Continuum* and elsewhere. His plays, documentary and short films have won awards and featured at international festivals. He has also directed theatre and circus and led the Circus Oz Living Archive project. David is Vice-President of the NonfictioNOW Conference, the leading international conference for creative nonfiction writing.

Tom Jackson is a research associate in the School of Media and Communication at the University of Leeds, UK. His primary area of research is sensory ethnography. Bringing together interests in cross-modal perception, anthropology, cultural geography and digital media, he proposes new sensory research methods. Through the design and development of digital tools, such as multisensory, spatial and participatory virtual archives and immersive and embodied audiovisual recordings, his work aims to explore the relationships between sensory experience and cultural phenomena. Tom's commercial experience in graphic design, photography and interactive programming have informed his largely practice-led approach to research.

Débora Lanzeni is Research Fellow in the Digital Ethnography Research Centre at RMIT University, at RMIT EU in Barcelona. From 2016 to 2017 she was Research Fellow in the Mediaccions research group at the Open University of Catalunya and in Information and Media Studies at Aarhus University, Denmark. In the past, Débora has taught in Methodology and

Media Anthropology at the University of Buenos Aires and was a visiting researcher at the Visual Anthropology Department, University of Sao Paulo, Brazil. Her current research focuses on developments at the interface of Smart City and Internet-of-things, the study of digital materiality, labour and moral order. Her publications include 'Digital visualities and materialities: paths for an anthropological walk' (2014); 'Technology and visions of the future: imagination in the process of digital creation from an ethnographic approach' (2014) and 'Smart Global Futures: designing affordable materialities for a better life' in Pink, Ardévol and Lanzeni, *Digital Materiality: Anthropology and Design* (2016).

Ann Light is Professor of Design and Creative Technology at the University of Sussex, leader of the Creative Technology Research Group and a qualitative researcher specializing in design for social well-being, participatory design and social innovation. Her current research relates to social justice, sustainability and sharing, with a particular interest in place-shaping. She also works on ageing issues, environmental and cultural change, human–computer interaction and how people make futures. She has led twenty-five UK research council projects and worked with arts and grass-roots organizations and marginalized groups on five continents, in local, transnational and international development settings. She draws on professional experience from the design sector and qualifications in humanities, arts, artificial intelligence and computer science. She is co-author of *Designing Connected Products* (O'Reilly, 2015) and advises the EU on the sharing economy.

Katherine Moline is Associate Dean of Research Training at the University of New South Wales: Art & Design, Sydney. Katherine explores the cross-overs between avant-gardism in visual art and the social pacts of contemporary experimental design. Since co-convening the symposium sds2k4: Experimental and Cross-Cultural Design (2004), she curated the exhibition Connections: Experimental Design (2007) and Feral Experimental at UNSW Galleries, Sydney (2014). More recent exhibitions for which she has led curatorial teams include Experimental Practice: Provocations in and Out of Design at RMIT Design Hub, Melbourne (2015); Experimental Thinking: Design Practices at Griffith University Gallery, Brisbane (2015); and Climactic: Post Normal Design at Miller Gallery, Carnegie Mellon University, Pittsburgh (2016).

Sarah Pink is Distinguished Professor in Design and Media Ethnography at RMIT University, Melbourne. Her research is interdisciplinary and brings together academic scholarship and applied practice. Sarah's most recent works, all of which have been collaborations, include the books *Anthropologies and Futures: Researching Emerging and Uncertain Worlds* (2017), *Making Homes: Ethnography and Design* (2017) and *Theoretical Scholarship and Applied Practice* (2017), the design ethnography documentary *Laundry Lives* (2015), and the websites www.laundrylives.com and www.energyanddigitalliving.com.

Shanti Sumartojo is Vice-Chancellor's Research Fellow, based in the Digital Ethnography Research Centre at RMIT University. She collaborates with a range of national and international colleagues in academia and the public sector, including industry-partnered applied projects. Her research explores how people experience their spatial surroundings, including both material and immaterial aspects, with a particular focus on the built environment, using digital and sensory ethnography and creative practice methodologies. She is author of *Trafalgar Square and the Narration of Britishness* (2013), and co-editor of *Nation, Memory, and Great War Commemoration* (2014) and *Commemorating Race and Empire in the Great War Centenary* (2017).

1

Approaching Uncertainty

Figure 1.1 A *Design+Ethnography+Futures* workshop commencing. Photo by Yoko Akama.

In a contemporary world where our hopes are ongoingly crushed by global politics and eroded by everyday life circumstances, uncertainty is often perceived as an increasingly prominent feature of existence, combined with imagined possible worlds of horror, fear and despair. These are challenging times. We are daily reminded of this through news of terrorist attacks, refugees and environmental crisis. Faced with such an apocalyptic moment the temptation is to seek a utopian future in which we might depend on tangible and ethical truths as a haven of safety. Yet the fact is, whether we pin our hopes on a better world situated in a time to come or pitch our fears into the terror of the next few years, the future is contingent, uncertain and unknowable. Uncertainty – however unwelcome and blamed for crisis, insecurity, vulnerability and indecision – is constant, ongoing and continual. Uncertainty is a way of being in and knowing the world that societies consistently seek to ameliorate, mitigate against, remove or deny – usually without success.

This book is for academics and practitioners who are seeking new and interdisciplinary ways to approach and engage with this world because we are tasked (or pressured) with creating 'better' futures together. This is often requested with impatience for results and outcomes. Society's desires for quick fixes and easy digest is eroding our ability to be resilient. This includes designers, anthropologists, geographers, sociologists, activists, policymakers and those working in cognate interdisciplinary areas and anyone interested in processes of organizational change. But what does future-making mean? How do we go about it?

The authors of the book are scholars in design, anthropology and geography. We practice along the boundaries of each field by blending, borrowing, hacking and remixing various theories and approaches to activate them in the contexts in which we work. A common thread that runs through all our practices is the interventions we undertake with people to generate insights concerning everyday phenomena. This might include exploring ways of using, responding to and making sense of mundane activities, emerging technologies or engaging with urban, social, spatial and environmental changes. Some interventions are intentional to catalyse awareness and preparedness for natural disasters or to build respectful sovereign relationships among Indigenous and non-Indigenous Australians. Others involve seeking new ways to collaborate with health professionals, local governments, cultural institutions or technology companies. Such work changes things, and we are immersed and implicated in these changes. As researchers and change-makers, we help people become aware of hidden dimensions, surface questions buried in deeply held assumptions, provide alternative perspectives and we ask what could be done differently. In such moments, we grapple with uncertainty constantly, whether it is our lack of understanding the extent of complex issues or our partners in the project who are often unsure about what they are doing or how to do things in new ways. Acknowledging that uncertainty, paradoxically, plays a disruptive and generative role in our work, as we draw upon an accumulation of our experiences and thinking, and pursue how uncertainty can be embraced by turning it into focused enquiry and exploration.

Through this work we began to ask, what if we take uncertainty and put it at the core of our investigatory and change-making practice? This book does just that. In what follows, we acknowledge uncertainty as being core to our existence, a dimension that cannot be removed. Instead of staying with its oft-negative association, we have come at it with a different attitude. We examine how uncertainty has been conceptualized in existing scholarship and practice and how a re-figuring of its meaning and potential might enable theoretical advances and new forms of practice and understanding. Most centrally, we ask: how might we harness uncertainty, to move forward with it into futures so we are vigilant of our blind hope for 'better' experiences when we are intervening in change? Uncertainty, we argue, brings with it possibilities. It does not close down what might happen yet into predictive untruths, but rather opens up pathways of what might be next and enables us to creatively and imaginatively inhabit such worlds with possibilities (Figure 1.1). This is not to deny that there are many forces in the world that invite us to imagine much less than meaningful futures, and we emphasize that this book is not a naive invitation to better world-making. Hope is not blind optimism, argues the activist and writer Rebecca Solnit (2016: xii), so this means we need to have our eyes and our senses fully open 'in the spaciousness of uncertainty' because hope calls for action. This action, we propose, is a methodology that enables us to consider futures and change-making as part of processual worlds of uncertainty and possibility. Here, by change-making we do not mean a solutions-based approach or formulate cause-and-effect. Rather we see change-making as a form of intervention in a process that involves the opening up of many possibilities. In doing so we create a theoretical and methodological framework for the engagement of uncertainty as a technology for the making of possibilities.

We tackle this challenge through a discussion of a workshop methodology (Figure 1.2). It is theoretically framed and structured, but open enough to itself emerge in different forms. These are shown through a series of examples, each of which brings to the fore a key dimension of the methodology. In demonstrating the workshop theory, method and practice, the book sets it up as one example among many of how uncertainty and possibility might be conceptualized and

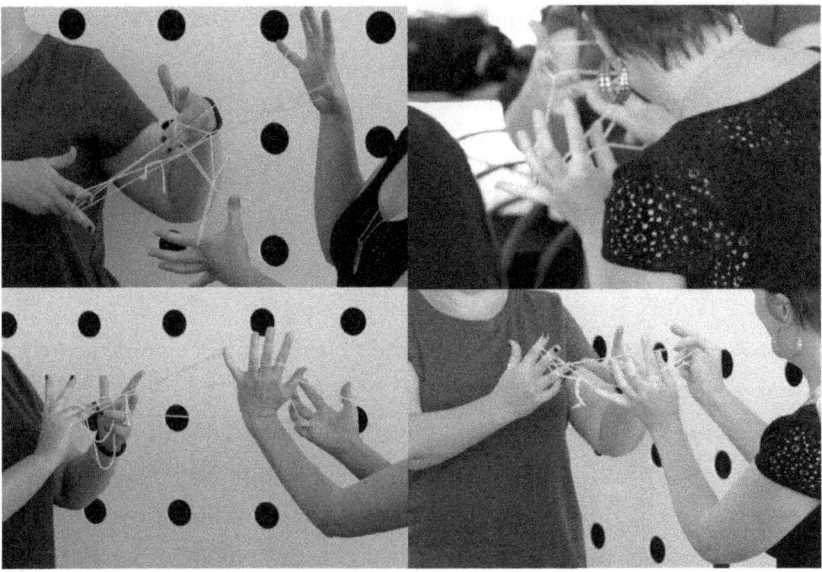

Figure 1.2 A collaborative practice as cat's cradle, performed by Anne Galloway and Helen Addison-Smith during *Design+Ethnography+Futures* workshop in 2012. Photo by Yoko Akama.

put into practice for change-making. We develop this specifically as a workshop methodology that combines principles and approaches from co-design, design anthropology and creative practice research to explore an interdisciplinary approach that does not cede dominance to the theory or practice of any one discipline. This methodology, we argue, is not only suitable for the development of participatory or collective workshop activities, but its principles can equally be applied to a number of change-making approaches and processes.

In this chapter we introduce the themes of emergence, intervention and futures that run through this book. In doing so we situate the workshop as an interdisciplinary approach that encompasses and blends perspectives and ways of knowing largely from ethnography and design.

Emergence and modes of engagement

At the core of this book and central to our understanding of uncertainty is an acknowledgement that we live in and grapple with worlds that are ongoingly emergent and changing configurations of things and processes. In such a world we have no basis upon which to be confident that we can know what will happen next in the immediate or far future, or that we can take any measures that could be absolutely guaranteed to determine or change our futures. In this sense both future-making and change-making become problematic concepts when treated through conventional modes of temporality. We alone cannot make futures because we are not dictators with perfect authority and power, or equipped with what is needed to intervene in worlds that are not known. We cannot make changes in isolation to the present because the present will not stay still long enough to be changed; it is always slipping away as the past. When we recognize that we are part of such a world, our only option is to participate more attentively in its changing. We can think of ourselves as moving forward with it, in ways that are open, responsive and with care. This book therefore does not provide a recipe for change-making, but rather offers a way of thinking about how we can move forward together. The central task of this book is to explore how uncertainty can be transformative, how we attune to and engage with it more attentively as part of our practice in change-making processes, and how uncertainty might be harnessed as a technology for producing new and open ways of understanding, making and imagining in the world.

In this sense, we attend to the possibility of what we call *moving beyond*. This is a useful attitude for us in many ways. It signals a pursuit of a future-oriented approach to explore what *could be* rather than what *is* or *was*, by speculating and re-imagining normative structures, boundaries and practices. But, it does not seek to predict futures that can be intervened in, instead creating many possibilities. Such attitudes are carried into our encounters when openness is lacking or not welcome. Thus, *moving beyond* refers to a willingness to fall into and engage with a possibility beyond our scope of tangible knowing and feeling. Possibilities are not closed products or even templates – they are instead open concepts, leaky and porous that have, and lead to, many starting points. Such emergent phenomena cannot be analysed or predicted, because they are not objects, but they can be attuned to and even welcomed.

Notions of emergence can be found in various forms within many existing literatures, featuring in dynamic systems from biology, physics and economics to organizational management. Indeed as noted by complexity theorist Jeffrey

Goldstein (1999), the construct of 'emergence' was a useful reminder for the sciences that always dealt with phenomena without perfect knowledge, yet contested as merely a 'provisional' term that was useful only until a better theory came along. Our understanding of uncertainty draws from anthropological renderings which are themselves derived from the practice in anthropological ethnography of immersing oneself in worlds where we do not know what will happen next. As Bill Maurer (2005: 4) explains, 'The point of emergence is that you do not know where it is going ... but to go along for the ride, in mutual, open-ended and yet limited entanglements.' The focus in much anthropological ethnography on following the processes, persons and things that we seek to understand is coherent with such an approach.

Both anthropology and design are fields that acknowledge the importance of situated, embodied and lived accounts, rather than those of a detached observer, and they see their positions as already entangled within and implicated in the sites they perform (Suchman 2002). In particular, in design anthropology, the notion of emergence has become increasingly central through the work of Smith and Otto (2016: 21–2) who emphasize that 'the present is always in a state of emergence' and suggest that 'design anthropological interventions might function to condense or accelerate time in order to explore and understand the emergent and the potential futures and imaginations it may hold or, in other words, to make virtual experiments on the emergent'. Echoing this positioning, Akama (2015: 262) describes how designing collaboratively with people (co-design) is to immerse in emergence and chance while attuning into 'slippery, un-namable tones and expressions that can only be sensed through our feelings and bodily encounters in relation to other people, materials, and entities' so that we embrace that we are creating, transforming and becoming together among this heterogeneity. This notion of the perceiver transforming while being transformed by their interventions and surrounding conditions is a significant ontological shift in co-design to articulate 'what it's like to be immersed in the moments of change and how this is constantly evolving and becoming' (Akama 2015: 264), going beyond epistemic conventions we often see in discourses of Actor Network Theory and Science and Technology Studies that only describe external and observable dynamics of inter-relations. This means in co-design, we re-situate ourselves in interrelatedness. The addition of the two letters of 'co' in co-design signals 'an openness to embrace the influence, interventions, disruptions, tensions and uncertainties brought to bear by other things and people. It requires the designer to step into the "in-between" space that is dynamic, emergent and relational' (Akama and Prendiville 2013: 32).

This emphasis on emergence and the relational creates a focus on liminal, ambiguous in-betweens of co-designing that Akama (2015) critiques are often left out in written accounts due to conventions in academic papers and scientific legacy that privilege empirical 'matters of fact' (Latour 2008), because such in-betweens cannot be captured on video or transcripts. In this book we propose a series of ways to engage differently with this problem, so that workshop processes that are acknowledged as emergent maintain this sense of movement. One approach suggested by Akama (2015) is to reinscribe this into our reporting through fictocritical writing and brief-but-vivid narratives. Following this, in Chapter 6 we bring together this idea of immersing in emergence and transforming together through the discussion of a workshop called *Essaying the FabPod*, led by David Carlin, a creative writer in non-fiction. This chapter unpacks the 'essaying' workshop methodology that was developed with another creative writing colleague Francesca Rendle-Short, and was enacted at the workshop for participants to imagine, encounter and propose new relationships to an existing architectural structure, the *FabPod*.

Chapter 6 illustrates the components of moving beyond. Uncertainty and moving beyond are perhaps more obviously represented in the creation of possibilities through creative writing. However, there is a strong argument for rethinking how the emergent qualities of photography and video can be understood as and engaged for more-than-documentation. These technologies are a feature of our workshop methodology and to the way emergence is understood. As Pink, Akama and Fergusson (2017) have argued elsewhere, a 'blended practice' that combines design documentation with video ethnography techniques enables a way of thinking about lens-based media that is not about capturing what is before the camera or to create a closed objectification of what was in the world. Rather by rethinking our uses of the camera as forms of movement in and through the world, we can conceptualize video and photography as media that are capable of acknowledging the uncertainty of what is to come, which is to open up the possibility of what is unknowable to us. This idea is based on Pink's earlier rethinkings of video as a trace through the world (Pink 2011; Pink and Leder Mackley 2012). This involves understanding video recording as a trace that a person and camera make through the sensory, emotional, material and digital environments in their forward movement. Following this understanding, when we view video we do not 'play it back' to see a previous moment in time from which we simply watch the unfolding of a recent (or not so recent) past. Instead we continue to move forward with that recording into new and previously unknown and perhaps unanticipated forms of experience and knowing, that is, as part of emergent worlds. This requires a shift from those design documentation and traditional anthropological forms of recording that are often too concerned with registering and storing what has happened, with the aim to have a record of a workshop activity. Indeed it is not only viewing previously shot video or images that requires a sense of moving forward, but also the action of doing video and photographic ethnography as conceptualized by Pink (2013; 2015) involves an engagement with the possible, since the video maker or photographer who 'follows' others does not in fact simply follow. Taking this further, we call for a mode of video and photographic recording that acknowledges the possible *with* things as they happen, and the ongoing emergent imaginative affects that are part of the process of making lens-based images: the visual ethnographer needs to ongoingly imagine possible immediate futures in order to direct the use of the camera. This understanding makes the temporalities of photography and video both more complex and appropriate for exploring uncertainty, and enables us to situate using video in workshops as a means to explore and sense process, as a mode of participation rather than a mode of registering what has happened. Chapter 4 discusses these experiences of using video in our *Spaces of Innovation* workshop.

In order to engage uncertainty for the task of comprehending both the worlds we inhabit now and to imagine possible alterities as part of change-making in an emergent world, we need a fine-grained account of how it can be operated. Incorporating theories of emergence, in Chapter 3 we develop this point further to outline how uncertainty might be understood as a *technology* (Sneath, Holbraad and Pedersen 2009), once it has been defined and harnessed as a generative mode through which to participate with others. This establishes how we might conceptualize uncertainty and the potential that it has for producing new understandings and forms of change-making. However our

Figure 1.3 Video and photography by Sarah Pink, Sarah Kushinsky and Yoko Akama.

aim is to go beyond simply acknowledging this potential and instead analyse how uncertainty plays an important role in our existing processes of research, making and intervention. Our concern is to identify how we might advance our practice by *attending to uncertainty* that can be used or harnessed to direct processes of transformative awareness and change. This is played out by way of examples from our workshop practices in Chapters 4–6.

Futures, interventions and workshops

The notion of intervention has long underpinned design (Kjaersgaard et al. 2016: 6), however there has recently been a greater impulse to explore the implications of design interventions in practical and conceptual senses. As Halse and Boffi (2016: 101) note, design interventions open up 'dialogues about possibility' and relate to 'people's concerns, aspirations and imaginative horizons'. Yet as argued by Akama (2015), impacts of intervention are often imperceptible, fuzzy, vague and dispersed. It is hard to articulate and demarcate change without the deployment of arbitrary and bounding categories. This is due to the incremental details of transformation that often remain hidden by their very nature of being silent, internal, layered, ephemeral, dispersed – all of which are difficult to capture and articulate (ibid.). Concurring with this, our starting point is that if change is fluid, ongoing, contingent and heterogeneous, uncertainty is a useful reminder of our own ideology and foolishness of thinking a desired outcome can be controlled intentionally. And perhaps the only option available to us is to be mindful of every tentative step we take with others as we attempt to move beyond what we know towards *what we do not know*. This means, echoing Solnit (2016: 4), we give ourselves to the future, 'and that commitment to the future makes the present inhabitable'.

This approach to intervention relates to an understanding of futures that likewise does not see what will happen next as being determinate or predictable. This is another useful reminder, especially for design. Design is one of the key disciplines that is focused towards and celebrates a future orientation. A definition of design commonly quoted is by one of the most influential social scientists of the twentieth century, Herbert Simon (1968); he describes design as a desire to change situations to preferred ones, which means that its orientation is always future-focused where 'every creative act moves to an outcome that is only fulfilled in a future, but, also, the outcome itself is a product for and thus is part of what produces a future world' (Rosenburg 2006: 7). The linear, discontinuous way of conceiving time could be seen as an anthropocentric mechanism devised to 'transcend the past' and leave behind error, damage, problems and suffering, so that we could 'differentiate ourselves and thus to absolve ourselves from responsibility' (Rose 2004: 17–18). Criticisms of short-term decision-making and poor considerations of legacy and sustainment seem to echo this deflection of continuous care and obligation (Fry 2009). Indeed recent rethinkings of the concept of future across the work of design anthropologists (Smith et al. 2016) and futures anthropologists (Salazar et al. 2017) point to a new wave of critical reflection on the place of design and scholarship and the need to align this to understandings of futures as ongoingly emergent, contingent and indeterminate. Similarly, many design researchers are equally troubled with design's obsession with the future, and the tendency to deliberately or unintentionally control, predict and prescribe how futures are made. Ann Light (2015: 85) reflects that 'designing is dangerous because it always projects forwards, but we are not able to judge where it will lead', pointing out how none of us, let alone designers, have the 'wisdom of hindsight' while 'continuing to exploit present futures with future goals in mind'. We share similar concerns, expressed well by Gatt and Ingold (2013: 145) about agendas that seek to 'conjecture a novel state of affairs as yet unrealized and to specify in advance the steps that need to be taken to get there'.

When design takes futures as its material, then, anthropology can bring a much-needed reflexive stance to interrogate the inherent politics to making futures in the present and methodology in impacting on them. Light (2015: 85) speaks to democratic participatory design as constitutive anthropology to explore alternative ways of being 'for multiple futures to be aired, shared and critiqued' as new relations between people, systems and things are created together, preferring to use 'future-making' as a verb or 'not quite yet' in her work to raise 'awareness that futures are mutable, undecided and co-constructed' and to 'create fertile ground for playful, pluralist and critical imagining'. Such notions underpinned a series of workshops under the banner of *Design+Ethnography+Futures*, discussed in more detail in Chapters 4 and 5, that were initiated by the authors Pink and Akama and others as a space to carve out practices that blend design and anthropology together, and also to learn alternative ways of being and becoming that place uncertainty at the core, and reflexively learn from enacting such engagements with others that are curious, hopeful and responsive. Like the anthropologist Hirokazu Miyazaki who explores hope as a method, futures for us is a 'modality of engagement with one another' (Miyazaki 2004: 6) to seed possibility and open-endedness and what has not-yet-become. This means that while coming from our disciplinary orientation, we are attempting to carve out places of encounter that are on the edge of, or beyond any disciplinary boundaries. Such approaches inflect how we use 'futures' in *Design+Ethnography+Futures*, not to see it as progress, a utopic vision, or to produce predictive, prescriptive steps in linear ways, but to improvise and embody processually by our gradual incorporation and supplication to one another and to other things. The notion of supplication as surrender is unpacked in Chapter 5. Haraway's notion of 'becoming with' was central to our workshops to see participants as co-researchers and companions in this endeavour, rather than fearing 'othering' that further separates (Akama, Pink and Fergusson 2015).

The series of *Design+Ethnography+Futures* workshops aimed to investigate how to facilitate a conversation, not on what we knew already, but about *what we don't yet know* and to strategize how to explore this together. Details about the workshop series are online at http://d-e-futures.com/ and we invite readers to explore materials on this site in relation to this book.

The workshop format is critical here as a site for intervention conceptualized above as an opening up of possibilities, and in this book we specifically explore the possibilities generated by a theoretically and methodologically refigured version of the workshop. The workshop is a well-established genre for the creative generation of ideas, insights and more in design and innovation contexts, often to the extent that it is assumed that simply by following a workshop structure 'innovation' will emerge (Berg and Fors 2017). Workshop type methods have long since been used in design anthropology, often involving the making of prototypes or the use of probes to generate deeper understandings (e.g. Sperschneider 2007) as well as in business or corporate anthropology and ethnography, particularly when this has interdisciplinary connections with design (see Cefkin 2009). It is a common activity in most design and business practices that have general features such as a facilitator(s) who takes a small group of participants (5–20, some have said 12 is a perfect number) through an informal, participatory and structured activity over a defined period of time (several hours to a few days) (www.wikihow.com/Run-a-Workshop). Its etymology comes from 'work' (study) and 'shop' (structure or shed for trade or work) (www.etymonline.com) that implies the purpose of learning through hands-on-doing, so participants engage in an activity together to share, experience, imagine or problem-solve an issue through intensive teamwork. Facilitators might introduce questions, 'what if' scenarios or a problem context to trigger engagement, or ask the group to make, perform, play a game as a way to work through an idea. Various methods can be used by the facilitator and there are numerous branded manuals on this (e.g. see Design Council n.d.). The general rule of a workshop is to have a sense of democratic participation, openness, play, experimentation and learning, nested within a specific context and often to achieve a specific outcome. Workshops can be seen as a form of praxis (theory + practice), and in design research contexts workshops are often used as a means to precipitate understandings of participants' perspectives as well as to co-create ideas and prototypes with them. This is also called co-design.

Another key characteristic of design workshops is the practice of design documentation, which involves careful record-keeping (through video, photography, models or sketches) as well as the collection and storage of materials produced by participants. As discussed already, while this type of design documentation has elements in common with ethnographic practice in that it produces materials about the things, activities and processes that have emerged, it is considered differently. Design documentation is fundamentally a generative act, as an abstraction of an idea, a crystallization of a concept, a trace of a tone or feeling in material or visual form (Lawson 2004). In contrast, (at least some) anthropological ethnographers analyse materials produced through research in an eclectic process, which is nevertheless always in dialogue with theory, and that creates connections between processes and things of different qualities and affordances in order to produce new and critical understandings of the issues in question (see Pink 2015). As Berg and Fors (2017) point out, there has been little critical reflection in the social sciences (for instance in sociologies and anthropologies of knowledge) on what workshops are or the kinds of knowing and learning they produce. This is partly because in disciplines such as sociology and anthropology the idea that new ethnographic, or ethnographically valuable knowledge might be generated through workshops, rather than through doing empirical investigation in field sites outside the university, would seem quite unconventional. This can cause concerns of meddling with disciplinary rigour, as evidenced and discussed in Chapter 4. It is indeed at the intersection between design and anthropology that we see deeper understandings of workshops and what they constitute developing.

More recently a design anthropology approach has been characterized by Rachel Charlotte Smith and Ton Otto (2016) as involving principles of emergence and intervention. They also emphasize how design anthropology involves 'defining and inventing the ethnographic field, and even to an extent the ethnographic subject(s), as well as acting situationally to produce various cultural agendas through the research and design process' (2016: 19). These encounters are not always referred to as workshops in the design anthropology literature, but akin to the approach we have developed and discuss in the following chapters of this book, their focus is on emergence and on how interventional practices can create forms of transformation, or as we have

Figure 1.4 Design documentations from the *Mindfulness and Technology* workshop turned into booklets and given to participants to carry forward the ideas co-explored. Photo by Yoko Akama.

called it moving beyond the knowable. Existing forms of encounter vary in scope, scale and intent, and here we comment on some notable examples in order to situate the collaborative workshop methodology discussed in this book in relation to what we regard as a growing movement towards generative activities that surpass both design and ethnography in order to create new ways of feeling, knowing and imagining. For instance, Smith and Otto (2016: 28) discuss how as part of the design anthropology process, participants developed interactive installations for a digital museum context through a series of collective design workshops with groups, seeing these as '*third* spaces' for the creation of 'alternative expressions between the digital lives of the teenagers and the research interests of the interaction designers' and as such particular ways of knowing. In another example, Thomas Binder (2016: 270) writes of what he calls 'the design laboratory' in which he and his colleagues brought 'together a network of collaborators with whom we simultaneously research and prototypically intervene in the everyday practices that they (and we) bring to the collaboration. We commit to this collaboration in the laboratory as an on-going rehearsal of possible futures.' Binder (2016: 278) sees these 'as *actuals* in Schechner's terms – the outcome of staged encounters in which the subjunctive "what if" touches on the real. Actuals perform the possible as a potentiality that becomes almost tangibly present.' These experimental and collaborative spaces like *Living Labs* (Bergvall-Kåreborn et al. 2009), Maker-spaces (see Chapter 4) and co-working hubs are growing in popularity across the world as part of a movement in supporting social innovation.

In common with these moves, the workshops we discuss in this book both sought to create new ways of knowing, and were staged encounters. They were developed in dialogue with three core themes – *Disruption, Surrender* and *Moving Beyond* – which are discussed in dedicated chapters below. While they are often experienced and structured as three stages, they are not presented as a linear process, but as a set of continuous, contiguous and often entangled currents that manifest in different ways in different workshop environments and circumstances. However, within this thematic structure and the staging of the encounters, space was left for emergence and serendipity. For instance the three themes of disruption, surrender and moving beyond, were themselves evolving throughout the workshop series as they bounced off a collection of other themes, but were the three that remained and were best able to accommodate the feelings that arose from our experiences. Likewise our decisions about which guest to invite to lead and facilitate the workshop was based on our relationship, their availability, willingness and curiosity for experimentation, rather than merely determined by their renowned expertise in their fields of research. This way of working allowed form to follow meaning through our respectful dialogues, as exemplified by design researchers like Watts, Ehn and Suchman (2014) where their project was influenced by personal letters sent to one another. Such an intensely collaborative process based on friendship and collegiality can often make it hard to plan and justify logically, but it reflects the candour and sincerity that underpinned all our explorations. As such, activities were developed through making connections between the ideas underpinning our exploration of uncertainty and the practice and curiosity of the invited workshop leaders. This was serendipitous in that while we planned workshops with leaders whose practice we felt was coherent with our interest in uncertainty, we did not know and did not seek to predetermine what the collaborations would inspire. This was informed by an underlying commitment to the 'what if' that motivates many creative practices and can also be seen as the basis of theoretical propositions.

The structure of the book

The first three chapters, including this introduction, set the scene for the following series of three in-depth, co-authored discussions of the development of the workshop methodology in practice, and of how these discussions take forward this book's core concerns relating to the generative possibilities of uncertainty. In Chapter 2 we unpack uncertainty and situate it in relation to a series of disciplinary literatures that have encompassed it, pushed against it or danced around it. Uncertainty has been co-inscribed with anticipatory concepts such as risk and associated with forms of creativity, journeying through different debates and perspectives that have lent both expansive and inhibitive qualities. Moving beyond these discussions however, we argue for a new rendering and mobilization of uncertainty as both a concept and an experiential category and feeling: understanding uncertainty as part of a generative process of the creation possibilities, and of ways of stepping into unknowable futures.

Building on this understanding of uncertainty, in Chapter 3 we develop a framework for using it as a technology for generating many possibilities. In ways akin to Halse and Boffi's (2016) focus on intervention, we propose uncertainty as a mode of interventional practice that seeks to invoke the possible through a process of casting off the assumptions that we have about what we might know, and instead moving forward in an ongoingly emergent world accompanied by ways of not knowing and of imagining.

Chapters 4, 5 and 6 draw from our series of workshops to demonstrate how we could mobilize uncertainty through disruption, surrender and moving beyond. Each chapter foregrounds one theme while also speaking to the others. The examples we discuss describe a range of approaches that were developed and extended in different ways according to the context and participants, ranging from a very 'loose' approach constructed in a participatory way by Yoko Akama at *Temple Works* (Chapter 5) to a 'tight' methodology introduced by David Carlin for *Essaying the FabPod* (Chapter 6).

In Chapter 4, disruption is examined to acknowledge both its contrasting, destructive and productive dimensions. This is a way to grapple with the untamable beast of uncertainty and develop strategies to reroute negative consequences of disruption towards enabling possibilities. This chapter draws from three workshops – *Spaces of Innovation, Myths of the Near Future* and the *Un/certainty* symposium. It details the methods that each workshop used in strategizing an expansive encounter through disruption, and also interrogates the uncomfortable experiences of the workshop in order to understand the structure, components and conditions that made it precarious. We do this as a way to signal what can often ensue when disruption is strategized and how to embrace and move with it.

Chapter 5 then introduces the notion of surrender that, like disruption, co-constitutes uncertainty. It speaks of the effort required in change-making that also means letting go of things like habits, control, expectations and entrenched ways of thinking, doing and being. This chapter draws accounts from a workshop that took place in an industrial ruin site called *Temple Works* in Leeds, UK, co-facilitated by Tom Jackson and Yoko Akama, where the participants collectively agreed to explore a precarious environment and trace their experiences of it. Surrender is re-framed, not as force and submission of subjects, but rather as a consensual willingness to open up to the environment, to suppressed sensorial experiences and to companionship. Here, the value of surrender is discussed as a form of a rehearsal in order to build collective capacity to be fluid and fluent when engaging in change-making so we may avoid reactive and defensive encounters with uncertainty.

Chapter 6 continues to pursue themes of disruption and surrender further, by subverting academic conventions in its co-authoring by David Carlin and Yoko Akama, who during the workshop invited the participants to explore creative writing as inquiry to produce 'an improvised experimental collaborative account of the uncertain cultural life and futures of the *FabPod* as of August 21 2014' (*Essaying* 2014). This account is 'risky', as suggested by the co-authors, precisely because of its unscientific methods of deploying irony, humour, metaphor and fabulation as forms of knowledge production of, for and with the *FabPod*, thereby moving beyond any conventional approaches. Here, the last triptych of moving beyond that constitutes the technology of uncertainty, alongside disruption and surrender, can be seen as an attitude, mindset or a method to insert into structures and conditions that may not have welcomed uncertainty in the outset.

None of these three chapters intend to provide a template for how a workshop around uncertainty *should* be done, but rather, through the examples of practice that we present, we seek to exhibit and engage readers with the possibilities that emerge from uncertain circumstances, and the principles through which these might be generated. The media-rich traces from each workshop should be read alongside Chapters 4–6. These are a series of three open-access online publications that we, in collaboration with colleagues who are credited in those documents, have developed in relation to this work. These are the multi-authored *Un/certainty* ebook (http://d-e-futures.com/projects/uncertainty/ and cited as *Un/certainty* 2015), which is particularly relevant to Chapter 4; the *Uncertainty at Temple Works* online publication (https://issuu.com/templeworks and cited as *Temple Works* 2015) based on the workshop that is the focus of Chapter 5; and *Essaying the FabPod* ebook (http://vogmae.net.au/works/2014/rezine02.ibooks and cited as *Essaying* 2014), which documents the workshop discussed in Chapter 6.

In Chapter 7 we shift away from the exploratory modes developed in Chapters 4–6 to draw together the practical and conceptual implications of uncertainty. While as we have emphasized, this book does not give templates for how to create workshops, it does however present a mode of considering and working with uncertainty. Therefore in this final chapter we outline these through reflections on inevitability, ethics, collectives, improvisation and emergences. We then discuss a series of examples of practical applications of the principles and themes that we have developed throughout the first six chapters of the book.

2

What is Uncertainty?

Figure 2.1 Hard hats – and obsession with risk. Photo by Yoko Akama.

Contemplating the idea of engaging uncertainty as a technology for research, change-making and intervention implies a rethinking of what uncertainty *is* or what it *can be*. It invites us to consider the characteristics of uncertainty, and how these can be refigured as part of a generative process. Much has already been written about uncertainty in the social sciences and humanities, and these existing literatures are coupled with colloquial uses of the term, which are also at play across different contexts and languages. Thus to speak of uncertainty as a generative technology also means to define or refigure it in a way that bears relation to, but departs from some of these existing uses. In this chapter we undertake this task.

First we examine how and where uncertainty has been used as a concept in existing research and practice. Then we look at how uncertainty has been defined empirically as a field of study, particularly in recent work that aims to address the particularity of change and crisis theoretically, but not interventionally. We then discuss how at the intersection between design and anthropology, notions of possible and probable worlds are becoming increasingly popular frameworks through which to consider how the not-yet-known might be brought to the fore.

The limitation of much existing research about uncertainty, we argue in this chapter, lies in its tendency to focus on achieving academic disciplinary objectives. A theory of uncertainty we suggest needs instead to commit to the idea that knowing is not only situated in disciplines, and that knowing is emergent from the encounters that go beyond disciplines. In this sense, the notion of moving beyond, discussed in Chapter 1, is not only concerned with going beyond what is already known through our existing experience of the world and the assumptions that guide it. Rather, for us as researchers and practitioners it involves going beyond what we know in our disciplines and the practices and frameworks that are agreed by their communities from inside them. It is this capacity to suspend judgement and to commit to a post-disciplinary theoretical 'what if' that we define and call on here, as being integral to a methodology which has uncertainty at its centre – and which we develop in the next chapter.

Uncertainty as a concept

Uncertainty is commonly treated as needing control or even mitigation. In this sense it is usually referred to as being relational to other concepts, and as a state or status that is potentially alterable, rather than as an inevitable, familiar or comfortable way of being. In this section, we develop an overview of how uncertainty has been conceptualized and mobilized for understanding traditional and contemporary societies, across the social sciences and humanities. This ranges from the deeply embedded anthropological interest in how uncertainty is treated in small-scale societies, for instance through mechanisms including witchcraft and oracle, to how forms of uncertainty emerge in society in times of crisis or global threat, such as climate change. It also includes sociological analysis of how societies develop particular orientations towards forms of uncertainty such as risk, and human geography approaches to the anticipatory modes of modern societies. We develop this discussion with a particular focus on how it has been developed in relation to its often-paired concept of risk in order to demonstrate how it has been given meaning, but also the limitations that this relationship imposes.

Sociological approaches to risk offer a particular vision of the world, which helps us to understand risk as a societal condition that bears a relationship to uncertainty. Indeed the notion of risk was at the core of some key sociological definitions of societal transition. The sociologist Deborah Lupton (2013: 17) suggests that the 'contemporary obsession' with risk is based on the 'deconstruction of tradition' and challenges to 'established thought, expression and practice' that accompanied post-Second World War modernity, situating these ways of conceptualizing risk as a result of rapid technological and social change which have their roots in modern industrial society. For instance, the sociologist Anthony Giddens (1999: 3) defined the 'risk society' as a reaction to an unknown future that will stem from a 'technological frontier which absolutely no one completely understands and which generates a diversity of possible futures'. Modern risk was considered to be beyond the scope of the individual to control, and as rooted in change driven by neoliberal capitalism and its technologies. Ulrich Beck (1994: 9) saw this as paralysing, describing how 'the horizon dims as risks grow ... with risks, avoidance imperatives dominate. Someone who depicts the world as risk will ultimately become incapable of action ... the expansion and heightening of the intention of control ultimately ends up producing the opposite.'

For some scholars the idea that risk was central to late-twentieth-century society and its interpretation endured into following decades. For instance Beck (2006: 330) considered that risk was a continuing characteristic of what he referred to as the 'human condition at the beginning of the twenty-first century', and it impacted on all aspects of society that were 'increasingly occupied with debating, preventing and managing risks that it [society] itself has produced'. The reflexive individual, who was seen as inhabiting such a society was risk-averse, constantly assessing risk and blaming powerful political interests for creating it (Tulloch and Lupton 2003: 16). At this moment the future held unknown threats – from global warming to transnational terrorism – that required action on a global scale to ameliorate the worst outcomes, but the individual was seen as not feeling empowered to take this action because the threats were manifested through 'institutions of modernity' (Tulloch and Lupton 2003: 16). Such themes have continued, for example, where risk has been defined as a 'codified social construct linked to misfortune, focused by sets of practices which channel power' (Gunn and Hillier 2013: 62), with expertise assigned to particular individuals or organizations. In this interpretation, risk as a concept transforms uncertainty 'into dimensions that can be acted upon' (Borraz 2011: 970). In these approaches risk becomes pivotal to society, however, the centrality of risk as a solution to uncertainty has been contested. Lupton (2013: 8) helpfully differentiates between risk, in which 'the probability estimates of an event are able to be known or knowable' and uncertainty, used when 'these probabilities are inestimable or unknown'. This leaves open the possibility of further interrogation of uncertainty as a different but related societal phenomenon to that of risk. In this book we pursue this option in ways that depart from the emphasis in the current literature about risk in three ways.

First we explore what happens when the starting point is shifted to keep risk in view as an element of contemporary cultures and societies (in varying ways) and to put uncertainty at the centre instead. The question of how dominant the notion of risk actually is in contemporary societies has already been opened for discussion. For instance, criticisms of the dominance of risk as a sociological concept identify the possibility that it might frame social experience in a way that leads to particular kinds of findings, asking 'what regimes of truth legitimate particular ways of accounting and not others' (Green 2009: 495). This suggests that in seeking out the impact of risk, researchers ask questions in ways that compel participants to frame their social experience in terms of risk, its mitigation and control. In this pairing of uncertainty with risk therefore, there might be undue focus on the risky nature of uncertainty. Indeed, sociologist Judith Green urges us to 'consider how far a framing of "risk" constrains our ability to understand or describe how people make sense of uncertainty in the world' (2009: 497), suggesting that as a concept it might limit our empirical understanding of social experience.

Second, decentring risk invites deeper emphasis on uncertainty. However this does not simply mean bringing what has been the sidekick of risk into view. Rather we explore how a focus on uncertainty as a transformative force might offer different routes, interventions and forms of change-making to those that follow from a risk-focused perspective. This un-pairing of uncertainty (from risk as well as any other concepts it might be attached to) enables us to reconceptualize uncertainty. There are two elements to this. One is the empirical and practical aspect whereby opening up to uncertainty may offer viable explanations and treatments for some of the problems and limitations presented by risk-focused audit cultures. The other is how working through a concept of uncertainty offers a particular vision of our world and version of how change happens, which we elaborate in the next chapter.

Third, another notable characteristic of the relationships between uncertainty and risk discussed above is their insistence on both as sociological constructs and as cognitive categories. As we show in the next section this emphasis has also continued through much existing empirical research about uncertainty. Our proposal is to turn away from these approaches in order to see uncertainty as an experiential category and a way of encountering the world, that might be harnessed for intervention. This calls for attention to how uncertainty is felt, affectively and sensorially, beyond cognition. This approach also foreshadows the workshops that we describe in Chapters 4–6, a methodology that we used to directly engage with uncertainty as a technology for collective inquiry. We discuss this in detail in Chapter 3.

Uncertainty as a field of empirical study

Green's (2009) call to reconsider the utility of the concept of risk cited concerns how framing a study with this concept predetermines the outcomes of empirical investigation. Empirical works on uncertainty likewise collectively suggest that we live in a global world of uncertainties and that the illusionary mitigation of uncertainty is inherent to governmental, institutional and everyday ways of being in a range of forms and across many contexts and scales. Indeed both risk and uncertainty have a certain empirical inevitability about them, given that they are both ways of explaining the unknown of what has not yet happened. Yet also in common in existing literatures, both are usually treated as unwelcome or threatening, and hidden by purposeful techniques for creating the illusion of certainty.

In some research contexts, however, uncertainty is treated as a viable element of ways of knowing. For example, at the planetary level, some of the most pressing attempts to get to grips with uncertainty concern global warming, climate change and its inevitable but unknown impact. Driven in part by scepticism about climate change and its effects, climate scientists have had to explain how they define uncertainty because it is so central to the scientific approach. As Gallant and Lewis (2013: n.p.) explain, 'in science, absolute 100% certainty is never obtainable' because of the possibility that new evidence could emerge in the future that refutes or complicates existing knowledge. Climate science is a fluid, accumulative field in which uncertainty might be quantitatively diminished, but never eliminated. Their explanation is closely related to chaos theory:

> All our attempts to understand complex systems and future changes come with uncertainty. So, we do not, and should not, draw conclusions from a single piece of evidence. We discern the picture of climate change by looking at all our puzzle pieces together. Ultimately, the only scientific certainty is uncertainty. (Lewis and Gallant 2013: n.p.)

For climate scientists, 'using probabilities to talk about scientific uncertainties allows scientists to communicate findings more precisely and transparently' (Lewis and Gallant 2013: n.p.), even if residual uncertainty can be used by political opponents to claim that the science is not 'settled' on the link between human activity and climate change. Thus, expertise is also empirically important. Furthermore, Morton et al. (2011) found that explicitly discussing uncertainty, an important part of scientific rigour, was viewed by the general public as compromising scientific authority. Thus, 'managing uncertainty is a key issue for those who are engaged in the process of climate change communication' (ibid.: 103). This is especially important because of the critical collective action required to address climate change, as more uncertainty led people to 'increased individual tendencies to act in their own self-interest rather than for the collective good' (ibid.). Indeed, research on climate change communication found that part of the danger of uncertainty comes from its potential to 'trigger confusion, disengagement, defensiveness and denial', and thus paralyse action (Morton et al. 2011: 103–4). One response to this has been to try to quantify uncertainty, rendering it more 'knowable' and therefore less threatening by attempting to come to grips with complexity and probability. It could be said, however, that because it is impossible to 'manage' uncertainty, and indeed because uncertainty is implicit in all scientific inquiry, what instead is required is the management of widespread *perceptions* of uncertainty as dangerous, frightening or generative of wasteful policy outcomes. Or, as we develop further in this book, to *re-conceptualize uncertainty as generative and inevitable, rather than as threatening*.

Critical academic discussion has however tended to focus on how ways of dealing with increasing uncertainty might derive from 'political mediations' and have 'less to do with the changing compass of risk itself than with its societal framing and deliberation' (Amin 2013: 147). In the context of debate in human geography, Ash Amin (2013) finds that different state regimes, and their national populations, have very different answers to the question of who is responsible for managing uncertainty, particularly in the form of responses to accident, disaster or attack. Tierney (2015) addresses this through the notion of resilience, which she defines as a neoliberal process that shifts responsibility for post-disaster recovery away from the state and onto the individual and private enterprise. Here, uncertainty is managed at the level of the individual, even when its effects occur at multiple layers and scales. Indeed, Amin (2013) similarly suggests that the treatment of uncertainty as ungovernable threat might be a result of larger neoliberal moves to individualize risk and shift responsibility for dealing with collective problems from the state to the individual. Such interpretations thus loop back to the discussion of risk in the previous section, in that they locate present forms of governing uncertainty, like those of governing risk, within the context of neoliberal regimes. Here, just as risk management has been seen as a means of managing the effects of societal phenomenon created by modernity, the management of uncertainty is likewise engineered to account for the uncertainties that are specifically encountered by individuals in their interactions with neoliberal states. Yet this account in human geography research does not show how such uncertainties are actually lived. That is, it lacks what anthropologists Saminian-Darash and Rabinow (2015: 1) argue is needed when they propose that 'it is vital today to distinguish among danger, risk, and uncertainty, both analytically and anthropologically'. By departing from earlier anthropological work which they identify as 'investigating how cultures cope with risks' they shift the focus onto how cultures 'attempt to create certainty' (ibid.: 1). Their concern is with generating 'a better understanding of the contemporary problem of uncertainty and the governing mechanisms it elicits'; they therefore ask 'how observations about uncertainty come to circulate in the contemporary world, constituting a new problematic field for which certain policies emerge as solutions' (ibid.: 2–3).

Saminian-Darash and Rabinow (2015) use a term that is increasingly popular in anthropology, focusing on what they call 'technologies' as a means to explore how cultures 'attempt to create certainty' (2015: 1). We explore the idea of uncertainty itself further as a technology in Chapter 3. However focusing for now on Saminian-Darash and Rabinow's conceptualization, in their work, technologies are used to do something with uncertainty. For instance, anticipatory scenarios might be employed as 'technologies' for the prevention of imagined forms of disaster, as in Adey and Anderson's (2011) geographical research on planning for civil emergencies. Inspired by Michel Foucault, Saminian-Darash, Rabinow and contributors adopt what they call a 'problematization approach' which involves taking 'technologies and experiences as objects of research and analysis and ask[ing] how they emerge in response to the problem of uncertainty' as well as 'what kinds of truth claims are advanced about the future, what interventions are considered appropriate, and what modes of subjectivity are produced within this problematization?' (Saminian-Darash and Rabinow 2015: 4). This typical anthropological interrogation of the concepts and of the ways in which meanings are constituted and activated in societies and 'cultures' offers a perspective, rooted in ethnographic fieldwork, of how uncertainty is experienced and dealt with across a range of relatively contemporary contexts. It differs from other disciplinary approaches, in geography and sociology for example, precisely through its focus on anthropological fieldwork as a way in which to research such questions.

Chapters in Saminian-Darash and Rabinow's volume reveal examples of how uncertainty has been harnessed as a generative force. Yet as we outline now, some of these forms of harnessing uncertainty correspond with the same values of innovation and growth that are part of the risk-averse institutional strategies critiqued above, and share a tendency to focus uncertainty into the domain of the individual, rather than embracing it as an element of institutional process. A particularly telling example is Eitan Wilf's (2015) discussion of how the uncertainty that characterizes jazz improvisation has been taken up by organization studies theorists to discuss organizational change. He argues that

> one of the key advantages of the incorporation of the jazz organisational template highlighted by these theorists is the fact that it is productive of an organisational structure that is not only flexible enough to cope with unexpected events but is also capable of producing unexpected events that can be further developed into and function as innovations in fields in which to remain stagnant is to perish. (Wilf 2015: 30)

Wilf discusses how in recent history forms of uncertainty have been introduced into certain types of organization and proposes that there has been a 'paradigmatic shift' in organization studies whereby it was realized that 'contingency and uncertainty have become part and parcel of the environments within which many organisations must function today' (ibid.: 36). Yet perhaps more significantly he emphasizes how 'the realization that some organizations must assume organizational structures that harness uncertainty into their very logic of operation, not only because they may help cope with external contingencies but also because such structures *are productive of contingencies* that are essential for organizational survival in specific economic sectors and fields of operation' (ibid, italics in original). These models of jazz improvisation have mainly been used in fields of new product development and innovation, where they are designed to create competitive advantage and with the goal 'to find organizational templates capable of generating numerous potential scenarios that are tested against the practitioners' expertise and knowledge of the market with the hope that some of them may eventually culminate in new products and innovations' (ibid.: 39). This, he argues, has had the effect of 'naturalizing ... contemporary work-related modes of uncertainty' (ibid.: 39) and precarity for diverse categories including blue-collar workers, investment bankers and 'mid-level workers in various knowledge-based companies who are expected to inhabit *creative uncertainty*', which can be seen as a form of experiential uncertainty (ibid.: 40, italics in original). It is regarding this mode of organizational uncertainty that Wilf calls for further investigation, including its potential to generate forms of anxiety (ibid.: 45). The implication is that the jazz improvisation model has the potential to harness uncertainty in productive ways, but that there are dangers in this – it is not necessarily always productive or beneficial to employees. Where uncertainty is harnessed as a drive towards precarity and anxiety in a context of neoliberal innovation and growth, the possibilities it can open up need to be critically interrogated. Our own aim in the following chapters is to develop an ethical and participatory approach to generating and harnessing forms of uncertainty.

A second instance offers us another way to consider how uncertainty might play a generative role. Natasha Dow Schüll (2015) discusses the example of how uncertainty plays out in the use of online poker software. This example is interesting because here uncertainty is positioned as essential to the game, rather than something that needs to be mitigated as in the context of discussions about risk. According to Dow Schüll, 'competitive gambling, in which action depends on uncertainty (without it, there simply would be no game), is an example of what O'Malley has called "enterprise uncertainty": gamblers approach uncertainty as a field of potential profit' (ibid.: 47). In this context then, she emphasizes the centrality of uncertainty, in that 'Although some poker software features serve to reduce uncertainties by turning them into statistically calculable risks, the preponderance serve to help gamblers abide and strategically engage with uncertainties that cannot simply be converted into known risks and to actively foster and play with new uncertainties' (ibid.: 47). She also tells us that online poker software 'serves to potentialize, rather than to minimize uncertainty' (ibid.: 48).

Dow Schüll holds up this approach to uncertainty as different to calculable risks, which are finite in that they 'occur within the context of a rule-bound game'. In contrast, she suggests that gamblers 'are experimenting with modes of decision making and self-governance oriented toward the open-ended indeterminacy of uncertainty rather than the limited, definitional project of risk calculation' (ibid.: 48), and this emphasizes certain values: 'performance over outcome, multiple data points over single events, virtual over real time, and potentialization over actualization of the self' (ibid.: 48). In this situation then, it is the 'poker-tracking software and its evolving array of features and functions' that become a technology through which uncertainty becomes viable, or something that can be lived with. This is because they 'alleviate this burden by enabling players to act confidently yet *without* pretending to know what will happen next. In this sense, the technology equips them to abide – and potentially to profit from – uncertainty' (ibid.: 50).

Dow Schüll's conclusion is that these forms of living with uncertainty are connected with particular contemporary societal states, in which online poker provides 'a testing ground for experiments in navigating the uncertain terrain of a world', where, citing Luhmann she suggests that 'contingency, risk and indeterminacy have become more prominent' (Luhmann 1998: 94–5). Dow Schüll (2015: 64) argues that the 'technological mediation' of the poker software 'neither tames nor provides refuge from perceived contingency; rather, it helps them to develop a subjective "readiness" for living with uncertainty'. Here 'the object of the game is not to master chance, but to master indifference to the outcomes it deals in real time and, in this way, act more gracefully and profitably in relation to it' (ibid.: 65). In this example therefore we see how uncertainty becomes part of a comfortable environment, where participants might flourish, rather than where they are seeking to mitigate risk, where 'they work to self-potentialize rather than to self-actualize; they expose themselves to uncertainty rather than avoid it; they seek to game chance, not to tame it' (ibid.). This possibility provides another related backdrop to the work we undertake in the following chapters, in that it offers an instance of how individuals, as part of a shared environment, might experience uncertainty as part of a situation in which they also experience the *possibility* of personal gain. These relationships between the individual and collective in the generation, experience of and action in uncertainty vary from the processes we explore in our own practice, yet offer us a way of conceptualizing the affordances of uncertainty as involving the chance to grasp, but not always hold onto possibilities that are continually emerging.

The anthropological attention to the detail of how different forms of uncertainty become interwoven in experience, imagination, technology design, discourse and societal institutions, as shown in these examples is important. Or, as Saminian-Darash and Rabinow (2015: 205) insist, 'studying uncertainties and their governmental technologies requires an analytical approach that facilitates the delineation of their complex formations, contemporaneous existence, and diverse conceptualisations of the future in concrete forms of life: that is they must be studied anthropologically'. While the disciplinary prioritization that their comments ring with is not completely aligned with our post-disciplinary agenda, the call to attention to detail is important, and is fundamental to how we approach the forms of uncertainty that we have engaged in the workshop contexts discussed in Chapters 4–6.

As we have shown in this section there is an existing medley of attempts to broach what is seen as a context of 'increasing' uncertainty, across social science and humanities disciplines. In common they understand uncertainty as socially, culturally and politically situated, and as a perceptual as well as empirical reality of contemporary nations. As we elaborate further in Chapter 3, in common, while they provide astute analyses of how uncertainty is present and how it might be explained, they do not consider in any depth how the ills that are associated with it might be dealt with. To propose a way forward, in the next section we explore how uncertainty might be approached differently. While it is no doubt a facet of contemporary societal configurations, and a feature of global inequalities, uncertainty might also, we argue, be considered to be a site for intervention, an element of processes of emergence, and as such an essential part of change-making processes, rather than something that change needs to be made to mitigate against.

The politics of uncertainty

Some existing approaches acknowledge uncertainty as an experiential category, and as one that is experienced in different ways according to the positioning of those concerned. In this section we explore the implications of this for the ways that uncertainty might feel and be *known*, and the power relations and the politics of expertise in which this is embedded.

Uncertainty is something that touches the body as much as the mind, as has been made clear in literatures, like that of risk. Lupton (2013: 641), for instance, adopts a related orientation to the scale of risk by treating it as a socially constructed product of individual experience in her work on public health:

> Emotion and risk interact with each other and in the process, configure each other … . They are each produced through other material and non-material phenomena: individual and collective memories and experiences, discourses, practices, objects, space and place, flesh.

Here, risk is related to perception, with individual decision-making based on both what is known and how people feel about these 'facts'. Assessment of risk is an emotional and affective process as much as an analytical one. This hints at the role of expertise when confronted with uncertainty, and the location of legitimacy to make decisions for groups of people – in other words, risk includes asking *who* is allowed to act or speak in the face of uncertainty, how legitimacy accrues onto these figures and how it might diminish or dissipate. Such discourses also raise the question of what types of explicit knowledge or embodied knowing about uncertainty get validated and under what circumstances.

Expertise is therefore an important consideration in how risk and uncertainty are empirically understood and manifest in the world. Borraz (2011) identifies the role of experts who assume the authority to identify and assess uncertainty and assign value to it as risky – in the case of climate change, as above, these are often scientists whose legitimacy rests on their specialist technical knowledge. Other 'stakeholders' in the definition and outcomes of uncertainty, such as business, government regulators and public groups, also position themselves as holding legitimate knowledge about uncertainty and how best to manage it. In Borraz's case study of mobile telephony, this meant that new types of previously 'non-expert' knowledge were granted legitimacy, including 'lay' or 'anecdotal' knowledge. Research into safety and health of workers in the construction industry and beyond in UK and Australia (e.g. Pink, Morgan and Dainty 2015; Pink, Lingard and Harley 2016) has likewise shown how formal and regulatory understandings of risk and its mitigation and workers' everyday practice-based ways of knowing about safety do not always coincide. This recent research has demonstrated that refiguring safety through embodied forms of knowing, learning and communicating can improve worker empowerment and understanding regarding safety (Pink, Lingard and Harley 2016). This shows how non-expert ways of navigating uncertainty offer viable routes forward. The shift and sharing of power from the authorities to the communities was also central in Akama's research into disaster preparedness in Australia, by harnessing dispersed knowledge that communities had of their environment and social networks for planning (Akama et al. 2012), though this approach would not have worked if the authorities did not accept the legitimacy of lay knowledge. Implicit in the widening of legitimacy was a recognition of the politics underpinning how a scientific problem was defined and potentially managed.

This finds a corollary in Pellizzoni's (2003: 328) notion of 'radical uncertainty' that questions the rational actor on which 'scientific-technical knowledge production' is based. He recognizes the political interests at play in constructing official knowledge, thus rendering such knowledge less legitimate and more uncertain. Here, uncertainty is generated by suspicion about the motives of the 'expert', and the erosion of the authority of scientific translators of immensely complex modern problems. Pink and Akama (*Un/certainty* 2015: 21) make a similar argument that uncertainty is 'something that goes beyond being a technique or element of research, design or intervention. Rather, acknowledging uncertainty entails a critique, it is anti-institutional, radical, risky' (see colour Figure 2.2). Their view on who can adopt and exploit uncertainty, however, digresses from a bifurcation between the holders of either expert or anecdotal knowledge – instead, uncertainty 'is operated from a position of confidence and privilege (by those who can afford to be uncertain, or by those who cannot but will take the risk anyway)' (ibid.). Sometimes indeed, taking the position of uncertainty requires a relinquishing or shedding of control, and endorsement of freedom and permission to move forward in ways that are less hindered by procedure, but that nevertheless entail a sentiment and practice of care.

Ingold's (2013: 110) conceptualization of 'expertise' through an account of storytelling offers a useful way to think about how we might move forward in uncertainty, as he remarks that 'the story offers guidance without specification', with narrators leaving a trace of their own experience for others to follow. Here, uncertainty is inherent in the transmission of knowledge, as each person interprets the knowledge told through stories in a different way that suits their purposes. The narrating expert does not control the outcome of her story, but still sets the parameters for the recipient to engage new areas of knowing. Thus uncertainty can help to de-centre 'expert' knowledge and process, as 'purity of method' is rendered less important than inclusivity and collaborative, iterative processes. Such an approach can yield outcomes that reflect the complex needs of 'lay' communities in ways that 'experts' would not be able to create without allowing the uncertainty of dispersed legitimacy of knowledge. Akama's (2015) work, for example, has used 'playful triggers' to visualize, share and build knowledge on local hazards and resources. Using such everyday objects to harness people's latent creativity, she encourages people to collaboratively explore how to collectively prepare for natural disasters in a workshop space. This takes us some way towards our main argument in this book, which is to make the case for uncertainty as *generative*. This approach accepts the existence of uncertainty and seeks to work with and through it as a powerful source of creativity and innovation.

In the next section, we address uncertainty's dynamic potential and value as a methodological orientation, particularly in ethnography, design and creative practice. Yet, there can be barriers to the processes through which non-expert ways of knowing become legitimated. For instance, above we have noted examples from Pink's and Akama's previous work that show how the 'expert' knowing and forms of creativity of both local communities in disaster contexts or vulnerable construction workers could be validated, precisely because they were invited into processes that sought to renegotiate expertise and knowing. However, as Sennett's (2012) work on collaboration emphasizes, it takes long practice to become good at co-operating. Indeed he suggests that real collaboration is a luxury of elites who can afford to invest the time and money in the intense, face-to-face engagement with other people. There is a complex politics of expertise that could see it accrue to members of society who are already powerful, even before this status is burnished by the acquisition of expert knowledge and the concomitant legitimacy to determine the limits or nature of the uncertain.

Uncertainty in research

If, as discussed in the preceding sections, uncertainty has been understood in various ways as a characteristic of contemporary society as well as integral to our ways of being in the world, it should be no surprise that uncertainty and its mitigation have also been associated with research practice. Indeed there are powerful parallels between the ways that uncertainty and risk mitigation have become procedure in institutional research governance processes through ethical approval procedures (Pink 2017), researcher safety protocols (Morgan and Pink 2017) and other regimes of academic audit culture.

These issues have impacted the conduct of research across a range of academic disciplines, and are particularly pertinent for those who, like in anthropology and design, practice ethnographic research. Indeed anthropologists have been particularly active in responding critically to these regulatory advances, and in doing so have specifically emphasized the place of uncertainty within their disciplinary practice (Amit 2000; Pels 2000; Strathern 2000). At the core of the approach to research practice that we advocate here is likewise an insistence on the idea that ways of knowing in research are not attainable or objective truths or facts that can be discovered by researchers who seek them out. Rather we call for an acknowledgement that knowing in research is emergent (e.g. Pink 2015), it cannot be predetermined and does not exist externally to the research environment. This is similar to what Saminian-Darash and Rabinow (2015: 206) identify as an 'anthropological mode of uncertainty', which is 'concerned with the logos, the logic and coherence, of the inquiry'. They argue:

> A mode of uncertainty is not a condition or state derived from a 'lack of knowledge' or an absence of the 'right meaning' that can gradually be overcome by additional information (description). The uncertainty we identify is an approach to a problem space; it derives from a form of thought and practice engaged with the capacity to define and understand sets of events, without which those events would remain a 'collection of details' or 'things in the world' rather than analyzable objects or concepts. (ibid.)

Similarly, many creative practices including some approaches to design, embed uncertainty in practice. These approaches, which involve working with the possible, the imaginative and the speculative, take an important step away from the imperative to certainty that characterizes some design research and practice. They entail an emphasis on 'learning through doing' whereby 'designing an artefact often involves serendipity, emergence, frustrations and unexpected discoveries – things that were never planned but encountered through designing' (Pink and Akama in *Un/certainty* 2015: 35). Ingold (2013: 6) describes this as the 'art of inquiry', a process of experimentation that follows what unfolds. It is a way of engaging with the world in which 'the conduct of thought goes along with, and continually answers to, the fluxes and flows of the materials with which we work', a state which he calls 'correspondence' (ibid.). Within this progressive state, uncertainty is present at every turn. Actors do not know what will happen with each new intervention, but they also do not know the complete extent or nature of the material with which they are working. As designers prod and probe a challenge, they learn about the limits, capacities and potential of the materials, people, processes or environments that comprise their inquiry. It follows that

> intuition and improvisations are a major part of a designer's trade (Goodman et al. 2011) and by extension, their dexterity in turning chance into an opportunity. In other words, designing by its nature has a great deal to do with being ready to act within an unknown, and for Schön, design 'hinges on the experience of surprise'. (*Un/certainty* 2015: 35)

Accordingly, uncertainty is at the very centre of design practice, animating and propelling creative exploration. This approach is not restricted, however, to expert designers. Sennett describes the vernacular improvisation that forms a response to ambiguity of urban form: people use shared front steps as places to sit, dry their washing and perform household tasks, for example. Here, 'improvisation is a user's craft' (Sennett 2008: 236), as people get to grips with their environments and how to get the best out of them. Furthermore, as with Ingold's work on storytelling, uncertainty in design is very often experienced and understood alongside others, and in relation to their views, goals, orientations and capacities. As Pink and Akama (Un/certainty 2015: 36) point out:

> the 'co' in co-designing is a signal to 'embrace the influence, interventions, disruptions, tensions and uncertainties brought to bear by other things and people' (Akama and Prendiville 2013: 32), even when incremental details of transformation are 'hidden' by their very nature of being silent, internal, layered, ephemeral, dispersed, all of which are difficult to capture and articulate (Akama 2015). Indeed, for design researchers who are often involved in assisting with the process of change, they acknowledge that projects are messy and unpredictable, often requiring agile, collaborative, systemic interventions with stakeholders (Akama and Light 2012). Designing in this space reveals the high degree of arbitrariness and emotions that shape the trajectory and outcome, and personal relations are strongly influential.

In co-design processes, the importance of the expert in determining the extent of uncertainty, and the best response to it, is decentred. Instead, uncertainty is part of a process that includes relationships among people, things, environments and ideas and that works through these towards design outcomes. Instead of disrupting, impeding or retarding creativity, uncertainty is absolutely necessary. In contrast to ways of thinking about risk or complexity that seek to diminish uncertainty, design as we understand it here *relies* on uncertainty and its generative potential. As Gunn and Donovan (2012: 1) remark, 'A process of design is thus not to impose closure but to allow for everyday life to carry on … [it] requires flexibility, foresight and imagination within processes and practices of designing' (see also Ingold 2009).

Opening up to uncertainty

In this chapter we have introduced and discussed a number of ways of thinking about, experiencing, dealing with, harnessing and feeling uncertainty. Embracing uncertainty involves acknowledging that we do not and cannot know exactly what will happen next, and engaging with the possibilities that this affords. We advocate this as an alternative to existing constructions of uncertainty as intimidating, unknown and precarious and to the search for means through which to control its potentially negative outcomes. In the same vein, we seek to evade efforts to govern uncertainty and define it as 'risk' or something that can be observed, quantified and assigned probability. This possible definition of uncertainty makes it coherent with our aims in this book to understand uncertainty as an ongoingly emergent and inevitable condition of moving forward into the unknown, which can be described but that must also be felt (and cannot be the former without the latter), and which is tangled up in and contingent on processes of action, experience and affect, and on the material and intangible elements of our everyday worlds.

Yet, as we have seen, not all attempts to embrace uncertainty fall within the same camp. The examples discussed above of uses of uncertainty to stimulate creativity in business contexts and the framing of online gambling through modes of familiar uncertainty are ways in which the uncertainty of some is used commercially in order to generate capital for others. In contrast, our aim in this book is to seek what we might call ethical approaches to engaging uncertainty, that is to use it as a route towards new possibilities for change that are transparent, participatory or open. In the next chapter we continue this discussion by exploring how uncertainty might be figured as a technology for this purpose.

The discussion in the sections above has focused on how uncertainty has been discussed as a societal phenomenon and an empirical discovery, and as a way to encounter the world as a researcher/designer. As we have moved through the sociological, anthropological and co-design literatures, we have also moved away from a focus on risk as calculable towards one on uncertainty as embedded in practice. Here rather than being a cognitive category that is necessarily imposed on participants or researchers, or a societal category for sociological analysis, uncertainty becomes something more experiential, visceral and felt. It is, on the one hand, a sensory, embodied and affective way of knowing and feeling, and in this sense we might define uncertainty as intangible and emergent. However, on the other, we also need to consider, if we wish to harness uncertainty, how we might define it in a way that is sufficiently solid to render it identifiable and graspable. In Chapter 3 we approach this question by conceptualizing uncertainty as a technology.

3

Uncertainty as Technology

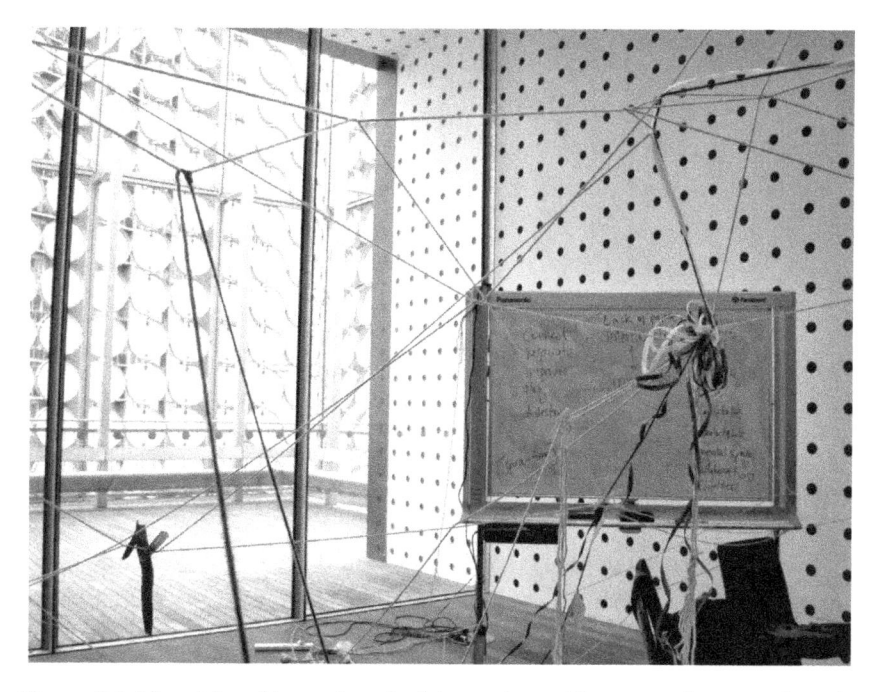

Figure 3.1 Material-making using playful practices with yarn and wires. Photo by Yoko Akama.

In this chapter we present an approach to engaging uncertainty within a methodology that treats uncertainty as a *technology* for research, change-making and intervention. This approach builds on understandings of uncertainty developed in the previous chapter. However it focuses on the re-figuring of uncertainty as a generative approach and proposes how, once harnessed as such, it might be activated.

The crucial difference between this approach and the existing understandings of uncertainty and theorizations of technologies in existing scholarship is that in existing work these have been seen as objects of *analysis*. That is, they have been treated as things and processes that can be identified as already happening in existing social and cultural contexts, that can be studied and unpicked, and that can be shown to produce change in the world or to inspire what might happen, or be imagined next. Examples of this include the empirical studies of uncertainty that we have discussed in Chapter 2, such as Wilf's (2015) study of uncertainty in creative work and Dow Schüll's (2015) discussion of how uncertainty is a facet of online gambling. Similarly while the anthropologies of technologies that we refer to later in this chapter offer us a mode through which to speak of uncertainty, they simultaneously focus on technologies as objects of analysis. These works offer a significant starting point for the agenda of this chapter. Yet while the potential of both uncertainty and rethinking of things and processes as technologies has revealed the generative potential of each, existing engagements with uncertainty do not consider how uncertainty might be *intentionally* engaged with to initiate or create fertile spaces for orienting how we intervene in our world. This chapter develops the potential of uncertainty along those lines.

As we have shown in Chapter 2, anthropologists who have been interested in uncertainty have focused on technologies for dealing with (other people's) uncertainty, rather than on the idea that uncertainty, figured differently, can be a reflexive technology in itself. The task of this chapter then is to turn this emphasis around to take up the challenge of asking how we might intentionally engage uncertainty as a technology. Our discussion is inspired by two main threads: Ingold's (2000, 2010) understanding of a processual and ongoingly emergent world; and the notion of 'technologies of the imagination' developed by anthropologists Sneath, Holbraad and Peterson (2009), which similarly emphasizes emergence and the indeterminate. Drawing these threads together, we outline a theoretical-methodological approach to understanding and engaging uncertainty as a technology. This entails seeing uncertainty as a capacity that can be engaged in practice *and* simultaneously as a way of thinking about the relationality between things and process and the effects that our use of such technologies might have.

In our experience, scholars, researchers and practitioners from across a range of ethnographic and creative practice fields see uncertainty as integral to their work. That is to say that uncertainty tends to be experienced and conceptualized as part of the practice of these fields of research, creativity and intervention. For example, as we discuss in Chapter 4, in 2014 we hosted a *Design+Ethnography+Futures* symposium to examine the theme of uncertainty. Our participants included researchers and scholars from across fields of art, design, anthropology, sociology, pedagogy and non-fiction writing as well as more interdisciplinary scholars and practitioners. The symposium had the expressed objective to work through notions of uncertainty together, and was also shaped to create and work with forms of uncertainty as part of its structure. Within this process we undertook an exploration of the place of uncertainty in practice. We invited participants' written and spoken articulations in relation to this – on postcards (Figure 3.2), in 100-word texts and on video, during the symposium. Their responses underlined the importance and relevance of uncertainty for all in processes of research, making and intervention. Yet, while uncertainty had positive, generative

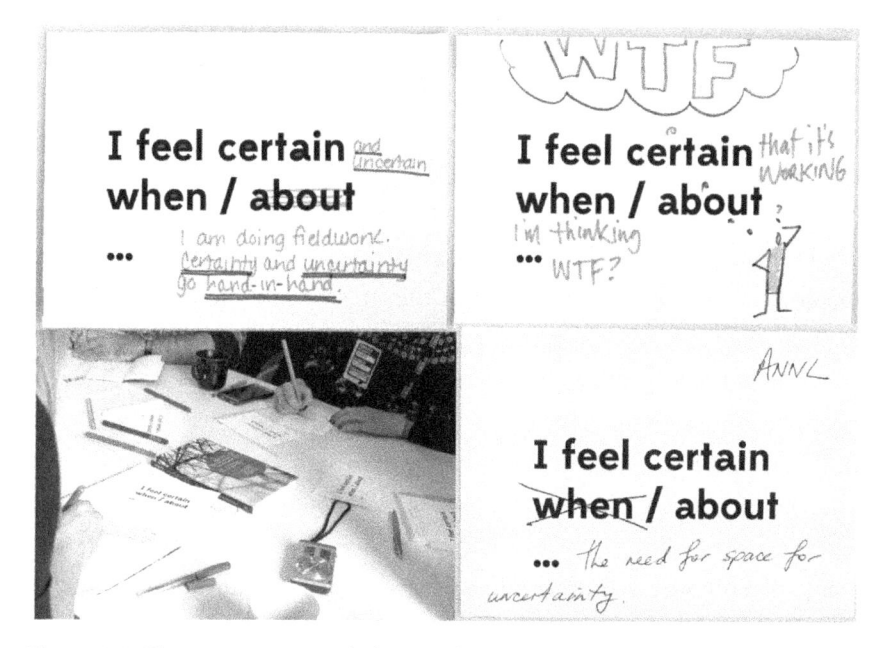

Figure 3.2 Uncertainty postcards by Heather Horst, Jeremy Yuille and Ann Light. Photo by Anna Farago.

and *necessary* presence for them, it was located in a range of different ways for different participants, in that it was dispersed at different points in the processes of research or intervention that tend to play out in their work. This event enabled us to comprehend uncertainty as embedded in practice, and as an inevitable and recognizable element of it. Acknowledging this, in this chapter we outline how uncertainty might be understood as a *technology* for research, making and intervention.

Uncertainty works in multiple ways across different contexts. As we have shown in the previous chapter, uncertainty has been recently, as well as more historically, understood as playing roles in processes of change, characterizing conditions that accompanied ways societies have evolved. That is, the empirical and theoretical study of uncertainty has chiefly occupied the attention of those who are interested in its place in culture and society. Yet, as we emphasized in Chapter 1, our own investigations have shown that it is in fact also pivotal as moments, feelings and states in research and intervention processes. While, as we have shown in Chapter 2, anthropologists have emphasized the place of uncertainty in the process of ethnographic enquiry, uncertainty as an interdisciplinary concept and feeling has been infrequently and inadequately reflected on or interrogated – practically or theoretically. Instead uncertainty more often remains implicit or removed, and might be explained away as part of what Law (2004) called the messiness of research, or reconfigured in ways that made it relational to certain categories like risk, which, as noted in Chapter 2, have implicated it in the audit cultures of institutional research governance. We take up these points to argue that we need to make the place of uncertainty more explicit, to attend to it as integral to projects that seek to comprehend the present and embark as change-making practices. Revealing how uncertainty participates as a technology of research and intervention, and how its generative capacity in these practices might be harnessed for change-making, is one of the core tasks of this book. In this chapter we establish a theoretical approach that explains both how uncertainty is made active in this process and how it is part of an emergent and processual world.

In what follows, we first examine what it means to refer to uncertainty as a technology. We explore the theoretical and practical underpinnings and implications of this, as uncertainty becomes re-figured as a *methodological device* rather than as just an *object of study* (although it will also need to be the latter to some extent). Second, building on our discussion in Chapter 2, we advance an argument for the ways in which uncertainty can be understood as a generative technology. In doing so we unpick the practical and theoretical ways that uncertainty is already activated in research, design and intervention – but not always attended to, investigated or articulated. We examine how and where the diversity of places that uncertainty is already acknowledged to lie in practice become relevant when we consider its generative potential; set up a framework for considering the affordances and qualities of uncertainty as a generative technology; and outline how such a technology can be an integral, *acknowledged* and *intentional* element of methodological processes for research and change-making.

Re-figuring uncertainty as technology

In Chapter 2 we developed an understanding of how uncertainty forms part of a processual understanding of research, design and intervention, whereby our ways of knowing in and about these processes are always incremental, often articulated verbally but also embodied, sensory and part of everyday unspoken activities and environments. While acknowledging this ongoing presence of uncertainty enables us to understand the indeterminate nature of what will happen next, our interest is in how we might activate this uncertainty to create possibility and change together. Anthropological theories of technology offer a starting point for re-figuring uncertainty as a technology. Drawing on a strong history of the concept of technology to stand for things and processes beyond the more common use of the term to refer to technical devices, Sneath, Holbraad and Peterson's (2009) rendering of 'technologies of the imagination' invites us to think of technologies in two ways. The first, they develop with reference to recent anthropological work on the Internet, to note how such works focus on the 'generative capacity of ... technological implements in relation to the social projects in which they are embedded' (2009: 18). Thus they set up the possibility to understand technologies as being things or processes that are generative and might therefore be studied as aspects of a culture or society. For our purposes in this book, such an approach can be applied to the different technologies discussed in Chapters 4–6, such as smartphones (see *Myths of the Near Future* workshop in Chapter 4) or an acoustically designed workspace (see *Essaying the FabPod* workshop in Chapter 6 and colour Figure 3.3).

However Sneath, Holbraad and Pedersen (2009) take this understanding of the generative aspects of technologies further, through a theoretical and anthropological understanding of technologies which is coherent and consistent with the theories of emergence that we have used to frame our re-figuring of uncertainty in Chapter 2. They argue, 'It is with these generative capacities in mind … that we posit technologies also in a second sense, which is distinctly anthropological. In addition to the colloquial sense of "technology" … we also want to argue that "technologies of the imagination" can be understood as a particular kind of theoretical object' (2009: 18). Here Sneath and colleagues explain that 'by technology we do not just mean systems of material tools … but a wider repertoire of objects and practices that bring about imaginative effects' (2009: 20). However they are careful to point out that this does not mean that particular technologies may have determined effects in the world. Instead they develop their argument with reference to discussions of the relationship between what have been called determinism and possibilism (Ingold 1997) by borrowing the concept of 'exaptation' used by Ingold (1997) to refer to processes by which things that have been developed for one purpose are 'co-opted' for another purpose. The concept of 'exaptation' is useful here because it goes further than the notion of 'appropriation' (e.g. Miller 2001) with which it resonates. This is because it not only refers to how things are used for purposes for which they were not originally intended, but also involves the '"refinement" (Ingold 1997: 119)' (Sneath, Holbraad and Pedersen 2009: 21) of such things. Therefore, Sneath et al. conclude that 'technological complexity, and its role in socio-cultural change, cannot be simply read off the material properties of tools, but is a function of the multifarious uses to which such artefacts might lend themselves in different socio-cultural situations – a function of their "affordances" [in a Gibsonian sense]' (2009: 21). They argue that 'as an intermediate position, so to speak between determinism and possibilism, exaptation captures a defining feature of technologies of the imagination' (2009: 22), and as such 'technologies "afford" imaginings in ways that, though hardly random, are nevertheless essentially unpredictable and often unintended' (ibid.).

In this way, if we understand uncertainty as a technology, then we can see it as generative not only in how things might come to be used in unpredictable and unintended ways. Rather, we can also suggest that when uncertainty becomes configured with other types of technology (rather than being simply a duality or relational technology for concepts such as risk), the affordances of these technologies in their configurations might change drastically with iterative uses that open up new possibilities for subsequent utilizations. For example, when, as we discuss in Chapter 4, a smartphone becomes imbued with uncertainty, because the parameters of how it might be used or shared are suddenly radically shifted, this opens up new possibilities for imagining through the smartphone the ideas, feelings and persons with which it configures. Therefore, when we depart from the tendencies towards seeing uncertainty as a threat or a danger, as outlined in Chapter 2, new possibilities arise: once uncertainty is unleashed from constraining concepts, such as risk, and once we stop seeking to mitigate it, or fill the knowledge gaps that it shows up, it takes on a new life. It can be recombined, reconfigured or made newly relational to things, processes, or concepts that are made 'open' to it, then its role as a generative technology emerges, and indeed is part of its participation in an emergent, undetermined world.

Two key issues arise from this suggestion. First, the question of what the affordances of uncertainty as a technology can be seen to be, and how these may emerge differently across diverse fields of practice. Second, because the ways that affordances of technologies might impact on certain processes, ways of experiencing, knowing and imagining are not predetermined, and engaging uncertainty as a technology creates something of a double layering of uncertainty. In the next section we explore these issues further through a consideration of what happens when we understand uncertainty as a technology of the imagination, and advance this conceptualization in a more practical and methodological sense, towards seeing uncertainty as a technology of experience and action.

Uncertainty as a technology of the imagination, experience and action

Like Sneath and colleagues, we are interested in technologies of the imagination, in that, as part of our original conceptualization of uncertainty in our practice, we aimed to harness uncertainty as a way in which to create imaginative renderings of possibility (as is discussed in the examples played out in the following chapters). As such our interest in uncertainty has involved treating it as a technology that forms part of a methodological process. Regarding uncertainty as a technology of the imagination means we are concerned with how technologies can be understood as participating, accentuating dimensions that are more indeterminate (Sneath, Holbraad and Pedersen 2009) in the making of imaginations. Sneath, Holbraad and Pedersen (2009: 24) propose that 'the imagination is *defined* by its essential indeterminacy, so that imaginings are distinguished from other human phenomena by the fact that they cannot be fully conditioned', then we might likewise understand the relationship between the imagination and 'processes that precipitate it' – that is 'technologies' (ibid.). For Sneath and colleagues thus it is only 'phenomena that are not fully conditioned' that can be 'conceived as phenomena of the imagination' (ibid.). This similarly means that for them '"technologies" count as being "of the imagination" [only] insofar as they serve to precipitate outcomes that they do not fully condition' (ibid.).

There are numerous examples of how technologies of the imagination might work, but one that is particularly pertinent here is that Sneath and colleagues pose that 'ethnography acts as a technology of the anthropologists' analytical imagination' (2009: 24). We would concur with this, in the context of what anthropologists do, however, in arguing for an interdisciplinary approach to uncertainty that involves a blending of research, making and intervention, we go further. We are interested in *uncertainty as technology* of the imagination, but also as technology of disruption, surrender and moving beyond. This means that uncertainty might be thought of as a technology of the imagination as well as of experience and action. We are, therefore, in a strikingly different way from the anthropological accounts discussed above, concerned with how uncertainty as a technology goes beyond enabling us to not just imagine, but how it invites us to *improvise, to change-make and to intervene*; thus it invites us to participate in creative processes that are likewise emergent and indeterminate. This shows how uncertainty is a technology in the sense that it is an engine of improvisation, emergent making and intervention, and a necessary animator of creative responses to the world.

Therefore, turning back now to the concept of technology, and taking the example of imagination as an indeterminate outcome or emergence that is derived from our relationships to technologies, we ask more about the ways that uncertainty as a technology can be brought to bear that *attends* to indeterminacy and emergence. Attending or 'attuning' (Light and Akama 2012) is a way that orientates our posture and senses towards a way of being, doing and becoming with such conditions, rather than a focus on instrumentality, which is often emphasized in the very use of technology. This is particularly evident in design, especially in related fields like human–computer interaction, which has interrogated and proposed methodologies to designing products, systems and technologies for use. More interesting for our argument is the emerging DIY maker-culture impact on ways in which the outcomes of design are 'hacked', adapted and re-made for different use by lay citizens to critique conceptions of technology's 'use as directed'. Some of these thoughts are touched on in Chapter 4 in the discussion of the *Spaces of Innovation* workshop. What could be possible during design-in-use and design-after-design in the hands of ordinary people has prompted scholars in participatory design to interrogate how the making of technology can leave visible the 'seams and scars' (Galloway 2007) to enable users to adopt an active, inquisitive and informed relationship to technology. If we take our smart phone as a typical example, its design has hidden its 'seams and scars' of its making to achieve a slick and smooth finish as an aesthetic of design, rendering it impossible for anyone to open it up for repair, reuse or remake. There are no screws or visible openings in which it can be dismantled without specialized equipment and knowledge. Preventing access is a way to keep users passive and uninformed in how the technology works and is constructed. This example usefully illustrates the ways in which Storni (2014: 163) claims how designers and design retain their 'power' – a 'magic trick' for exclusive control and proprietary knowledge, questioning 'what can be done (during design) in order to open up the possibility of users taking power on their own initiative (after design)'. This discussion brings our focus to the way we 'make' the technology is as important as what technology can do in its 'use' by people to ensure that avenues for possibility can continue to remain open.

Taking these ideas further into the arena of uncertainty, we initially break technology down further to examine its 'seams and scars', following Galloway (2007) and Storni (2014), in producing the kinds of uncertainty we observed, experienced and encountered in the *Design+Ethnography+Futures* workshops. The 'seams and scars' that constitute technology of uncertainty are offered for discussion below and in Chapters 4–6 – those of disruption, surrender and moving beyond. In this rendering the relationship between uncertainty on the one hand, and the three concepts of disruption, surrender and moving beyond on the other, is one of mutuality. By this we mean that while we see uncertainty as the technology through which we might create circumstances that are characterized by the categories of disruption, surrender and moving beyond, these categories are simultaneously constitutive of uncertainty. We also emphasize that these categories are mobilized in a particular way in this book, since they are actioned in practical ways through a workshop modality, as is demonstrated in the following chapters. The discussions in these chapters bring to the fore a series of affordances that are enabled when uncertainty is employed as a technology. They are of course not the only affordances that can be associated with this process, but they are put forward here as examples of evocative and actual ways that uncertainty as a technology has made possible particular forms and modes of experiencing, being and action, that can be practically shaped.

Uncertainty as technology for disruption

Disruption is a strategy that has been rehearsed in creative practice and scholarly research enquiry in processes of defamiliarization and making strange. Modes of unsettling our assumptions and opening up to new ways of knowing, seeing or thinking have informed approaches in anthropology and design. For instance, according to Bell, Blythe and Sengers (2005), making strange originated in the early twentieth century as a technique to avoid 'habitual recognition' in order to observe and experience phenomena anew. For example, until the late twentieth century, 'anthropology at home' movement (e.g. Amit 2000; Okely 1996), anthropologists in the British tradition tended to travel overseas to learn a culture and language they had little or no prior experience of, in order to gain understandings that would be impossible within their 'own' familiar culture. While ethnography 'at home' was subsequently justified following the logic that in non-homogenous cultures, there would always be as yet unencountered fieldwork contexts requiring cultural learning, such assumptions do not advance our thought about what anthropological ethnography can be. Instead recent literatures in anthropology and design anthropology have emphasized doing ethnography *with* research participants rather than *about* them (Ingold 2010) and ethnographers working *with* designers, rather than studying them or doing studies to inform design (Anusas and Harkness 2016). Therefore we understand an ethnographic sensibility as the capacity to look beneath the surface of what is visible and verbalized, in collaboration *with* research participants and partners, even in contexts very familiar to the researcher. In this sense disruption is concerned with breaking through the surface, disregarding what we think is happening, and abandoning or putting into suspension what we think we know, or believe we can be certain of, in order to delve deeper into the sensory and emotional states that are entailed in the activities, relations, materialities and environments of the everyday (e.g. Pink 2015). This ethnographic sensibility moreover spills into interdisciplinary collaborations whereby ethnographers do not simply supply materials to design disciplines, but allows the practices of design and ethnography to leak and seep into each other. The underpinning assumption in this approach is that things always exceed what they superficially appear to be and that we might encounter this excess by inviting participants and research collaborators to journey with us into new ways of questioning what is happening, what can be imagined and what is possible. As Light (2015) argues, the act of bringing people together to experience their differences at close range allows for a constitutive anthropology, where new ways of knowing about the world can be uniquely found in line with other performative understandings of intersubjectivity.

This revised ethnographic approach and sensibility corresponds with avant-garde movements in art and design, such as Dada, Situationists and

Deconstructionists, where objects, environments and performances were designed to 'carve alternative cultural spaces for ambiguity, play, humour, critique, provocation, debate, imagining and creativity' (Akama, Stuedahl and Van Zyl 2015: 133). There is also, in participatory design, a rich history that strategizes 'breakdowns' as a generative way to manifest and deal with conflict and contradictions among participants. For example, Bødker et al. (1991) observe how breakdowns can trigger ways to re-examine, re-focus and re-shift approaches taken for granted, and offer rich learning experiences and new insights for exploration. These disruptions can surface contradictions and promote friction to reveal phenomena and agendas previously hidden from view. Such breakdowns include unexpected and serendipitous change in agenda, focus or situations within the contingent nature of participatory action research, often demanding a reflexive, open, candid approach for all (including research participants) to learn from.

This lineage indicates why design is still performing techniques of generative disruptions, most recognizably in fields or movements like Critical Design and Speculative Design. Disruption is explicitly pursued here, for example, in objects and performances that take the form of fictional and absurd future projections to ask difficult and ignored questions and to provoke and disturb common understandings (Dunne and Raby 2013; Michael 2012). Art, interaction design and research duo Tony Dunne and Fiona Raby (2001; 2013) are widely celebrated for their works that provoke questions and reveal issues of the socio-technical world. Here, objects are not designed to perform certain functions or satisfy user needs – the usual expectation of design – instead, the object (or design) provoke and interrogate our engagement with technology and futures. These range from 'Placebo objects' (Dunne and Raby 2001) that were placed in people's homes for personal interrogation of familiar environments, or as hypothetical exhibits in art galleries that challenge assumptions and provoke new imaginings and relationships (Dunne and Raby 2013). Yet, what may still be elusive in these examples, which prefer to make strange 'other' people's socio-technical worlds, is the anthropological reflexivity that interrogates the creators' (i.e. the designers') own positionality, accountability, world view and value systems. This is a common critique of design, most prominently pointed out by anthropologist Lucy Suchman, who discusses the prevalence of the view of 'design from nowhere' by 'anonymous and unlocatable designers' that is often encouraged in professional design (2002: 95).

These forms of disruption are all concerned with seeking to shift our ways of understanding what is visible and to dissolve the sense of certainty that is based in what we think we know. Our workshop methodology had an undercurrent to disrupt the instigators (also co-facilitators of the workshops) to scaffold activities that fostered unintentionality as opposed to intentionality, and create opportunities for uncertainty and the possibilities that would emerge from it, instead of achieving certainty. This was uncharted waters and a confusing experience for many, including Yoko and Sarah as instigators and the guest facilitators they invited to run the series of workshops. It was no surprise that several workshops resulted in some of the participants leaving part-way, or showing and expressing discomfort. These forms of discomfort are understood differently from those discussed in Chapter 2 (for example, in making creative workers precarious to stimulate creativity) and are interpreted as an augmentation of the presence of uncertainty, by foregrounding the inevitability of not knowing.

In Chapter 4 we pursue these uses of disruption as a technology through a discussion of a series of *Design+Ethnography+Futures* workshops in which disruption was an inevitable element of our process of moving forward with participants: The *Spaces of Innovation* workshop, led by Dèbora Lanzeni and Elisenda Ardèvol, which intentionally sought to disrupt participants' modes of thinking and doing though inviting engagement with principles and temporalities of the maker movement; and the *Myths of the Near Future* workshop led by Katherine Moline (see Akama, Moline and Pink 2016) which explored ideas of making the familiar strange to facilitate new perspectives on technologies taken for granted in changing media ecologies, where disruption activated in a more abrupt and explicit way when Moline invited the participants to swap their phones with strangers to see what the interaction revealed about each other and themselves (see colour Figure 3.4).

Chapter 6 examines another way in which disruption as an affordance of uncertainty was developed, in this case through a structured approach that was designed to both reveal and dispel our existing assumptions about an acoustically attuned architect-designed meeting space, the *FabPod*, by creating a deliberative 'disruption' – and to examine the ways we (ethnographers, designers, architects and research participants) can know or not know. The documentation process for this event was undertaken differently, by a vlog expert Adrian Miles, and led to a publication, which also reflected the structure of the process (see Carlin et al. 2015; *Essaying* 2014).

Uncertainty as technology for surrender

If the technology of disruption is seen as a trigger and provocation to re-orientate our posture and frame, then a technology for surrender works similarly to what meditation can often enable by embarking on ways to discard the 'space suit' padded with 'habits and preconceptions, the armour with which one habitually distances oneself from one's experience' (Varela, Thompson and Rosch 1993: 25). The notion of surrendering may seem problematic and contradictory to the usual purposes of research and scholarship, which is to generate and gain new knowledge. It is common to argue, defend, evidence and build expertise as a form of mastery, specialism and distinction in a field. Yet technology for surrender could be seen as a different sense of effort as acts of *unlearning* rather than learning (Varela, Thompson and Rosch 1993) that counters prescriptive approaches as a way of mitigating uncertainty. In a combative frame and logic of power and political structures, surrender can be interpreted to mean 'defeat' or 'victimize' as a result of disempowerment. Instead, surrender used in our discussion is shaped by various philosophies of intimacy (Kasulis 2002), empathy (Mccarthy 2010) and mindfulness (Akama 2018), where plurality is irreducible to the singular 'I' that does not precede the relation of 'we' (Nancy 2000). In other words, we adopt a feminist, co-ontological approach that already assumes connection and interdependency of all beings and non-beings, where independent identities and boundaries erode and 'each surrenders part of its own nature' (Kasulis 2002: 54) as a 'movement of incorporation rather than inscription' (Ingold 1993: 157) to acknowledge and become part of the continual world's transformation. Thus, the way we conceive surrender is a movement that molts sharp distinctions, towards further intimacy and participation with our world.

When uncertainty is constituted through technology of surrender, we can begin to appreciate that disruptions and serendipity can also aid change-making, rather than selectively attributing purposeful change as a result of our interventions. Errors, accidents and failures must be embraced as a possibility from the outset, requiring a readiness for contingency, rather than controlling ways to mitigate them. Contingency is already acknowledged and documented in the fields of design and anthropology as necessary to embrace (e.g. Salazar et al. 2017; Smith et al. 2016), rather than control or eliminate. Scholars in design anthropology describe the need to surrender to the flux and flow of change as a necessary process of transformation to untether and dismantle the safety of competence and 'confront security and comfort of existing knowledge in order to pursue a risky and discomforting change process' (Akama, Stuedahl and Van Zyl 2015: 142).

Surrender is not always uniform or easy to accomplish. For example, *Temple Works* workshop in Chapter 5 best illustrates how the experience teetered on a knife-edge of precariousness and creativity. Here participants collectively explored the 'undercroft' space beneath the former flax mill, despite explicit request not to go there by Tom Jackson, the host and co-facilitator. He had to surrender to the group's desire and negotiate his own anxiety and responsibility as the host. There were stories of people getting lost in the dark, labyrinthine passages. If the workshop had not been centred on exploring uncertainty, perhaps the participants may not have attempted this adventure. The reflection by the host and co-explorers reveals confronting acts that heightened visceral discomfort and thrill resulting from imagined and sensually deprived encounters. Of interest here is how the group negotiated ways to balance safety and harm, which was configured differently depending on the individual's proximity to risk as the collective exploration in the undercroft took place. For many, this exploration became a way that interrogated how they cope with anxiety, vulnerability and uncertainty, to reflexively see what they were able to surrender and what they could open themselves up to. By holding hands and communicating their collective senses to one another through whispers, intake of breath or touch, there was a powerful demonstration of trust and intimacy as well as suggestion of a surrender of the self to one another.

Surrender was also in play in the collective exploration of the *FabPod*, detailed in Chapter 6. The participants in a workshop were invited to embark on what was for some an unknown mode of investigating by means of creative non-fiction writing. This entailed a form of surrendering to the process of inquiry without knowing if the task could be completed, or even be adequate. Behind this anxiety lurked a real vulnerability to being unable to demonstrate eloquence or even have the words to imagine the *FabPod* in a completely new way. Here uncertainty fuelled both creativity and a frisson of anxiety, and surrendering to this was required to move forward through each structured writing task and remain open to the process.

Technology for surrender can test the limits to our own willingness for uncertainty and openness that are often configured by a contingent context. As Debora Bird Rose (2004: 22), a celebrated anthropologist who works with Indigenous Australians, explains, 'Openness is risky because one does not know the outcome. To be open is to hold one's self available to others: one takes risks and becomes vulnerable. But this is also a fertile stance: one's own ground can become destabilized. In open dialogue one holds one's self available to be surprised, to be challenged, and to be changed.' Surrender and openness are twin concepts because risk, vulnerability and disruption do not come about by holding on to certainties of power, knowledge or truths. These must be surrendered before any state of openness can be arrived at.

As a possible affordance of bringing to the fore different manifestations of uncertainty, surrender was embraced and willingly pursued in *Design+Ethnography+Futures* workshops as a provocation to us all (participants and facilitators) to 'let go' of our preconceptions, forego the need for resolution, and step out of our respective disciplinary certainties to consider alternative approaches and experiment with what might emerge out of an assembly of ideas, people and things. One could almost suggest that the workshops were intentionally designed for us to rehearse how to attune, sensitize and become mindful towards the emergent unknowns. When uncertainty can encourage fear for each other, neighbours and strangers, the workshop worked as a way to reverse this – to trust in one another as the only way forward. As we shall hear, embracing uncertainty often triggered genuine surprise and reconfigured ways of being and knowing collaboratively, and in the following chapters we explore in more depth how this can be achieved in practice and the possibilities this can open up.

Uncertainty as technology for moving beyond

In the discussion above we have suggested how uncertainty can be engaged as a technology for disruption and surrender, following from this we now consider the third affordance of uncertainty that pertains to our process – that of moving beyond. Moving beyond is a key element of our goal to harness uncertainty for the generation of possibility because it stands for the moments and experiences of encounter with what we do not or cannot (yet or ever) know, with that which has not occurred but that emerges as part of our horizons of hope and fear and that occupies the world of the possible. It is through these encounters with the possible that we learn to live in and navigate through the not-yet-known as it ongoingly emerges. The use of uncertainty as a technology for moving beyond is therefore a process that generates both imaginative and anticipatory ways of understanding what might be next, and assists us in stepping over into both our immediate futures and in making proposals for future actions.

Moving beyond also carries 'responsibilities' of how and what we are moving towards. Since the future is not a predetermined place or location, then we cannot see it as if it were a landing site that we will collectively end up in. Rather this 'where' needs to be understood as plural, contested and contingently created, and we should keep in mind that while we can imagine, and while discourses of risk and its mitigation are often created in relation to this as discussed in Chapter 2, we can never actually know where we are going. Heeding Rose (2004), this might mean we do not simply 'move beyond' by forgetting the past but we also re-engage with the wisdom and lived experiences of elders, and philosophies of resilience, survival, endurance that co-evolved through centuries of human evolution and suffering.

In the forthcoming chapters, we address the question of moving beyond in several ways. These are united by our aim to develop ways of moving beyond that enable the possible to emerge, and to invite imaginative ways of encountering indeterminate futures in the present. As our discussions of workshop processes and techniques also reveal, this stage of the process is also a deliberately shaped activity on the part of workshop conveners. For example, the creating of uncertainty for the generation of disruptions is a simpler action that involved inviting people to disengage from the familiar in ways that might lead to more chaotic or messy environments, sequences of activity or emotions. However in contrast, moving beyond was more closely convened and structured, participants were invited to engage in activities in which rather than having what was already meaningful swept from under their feet, the workshop process created a scaffolding upon which they could stand and a set of resources through which they might create possibilities. For example in the *Myths of the Near Future* workshop (Chapter 4), while disruptions to the norms of smartphone sharing created senses of discomfort, the processes of building new technologies that people were later invited into enabled them to go beyond existing smartphone technologies in imaginative ways. Similarly as outlined in Chapter 6 when participants in our *FabPod* workshop were asked to create stories about the future *FabPod*, they did so on the basis of collectively constituted resources of knowledge about it. This knowledge was not necessarily meant to be objectively true, but was rather a resource that was made because the group was able to surrender to the sharing of co-produced knowing that emerged from our circumstances, as discussed above. It was by surrendering in this way that the possibilities of going beyond came about.

A guide to reading the following chapters

In this chapter we have explained how uncertainty can be re-figured as a technology for developing generative forms of disruption, surrender and moving beyond. We see these three processes as integral to the research, change-making and interventions that we are interested in. In the following chapters we demonstrate how through a series of workshops we have developed, applied and honed these processes. They are not however presented as strategies for readers to repeat as methods or approaches. Instead we share them as an example of how a workshop methodology and series has evolved and consolidated as a coherent set of themes and principles. We offer this methodology to readers as a possibility to work with, that might be used to inspire and catalyse new ways into uncertainty. That is to develop techniques of research and intervention that are appropriate to undermine other certainties, in ways that are productive and generative, and that might catalyse further thinking on change-making.

4

Strategies for Disruption

Yoko Akama, Sarah Pink, Dèbora Lanzeni, Elisenda Ardèvol, Katherine Moline, Ann Light and Shanti Sumartojo

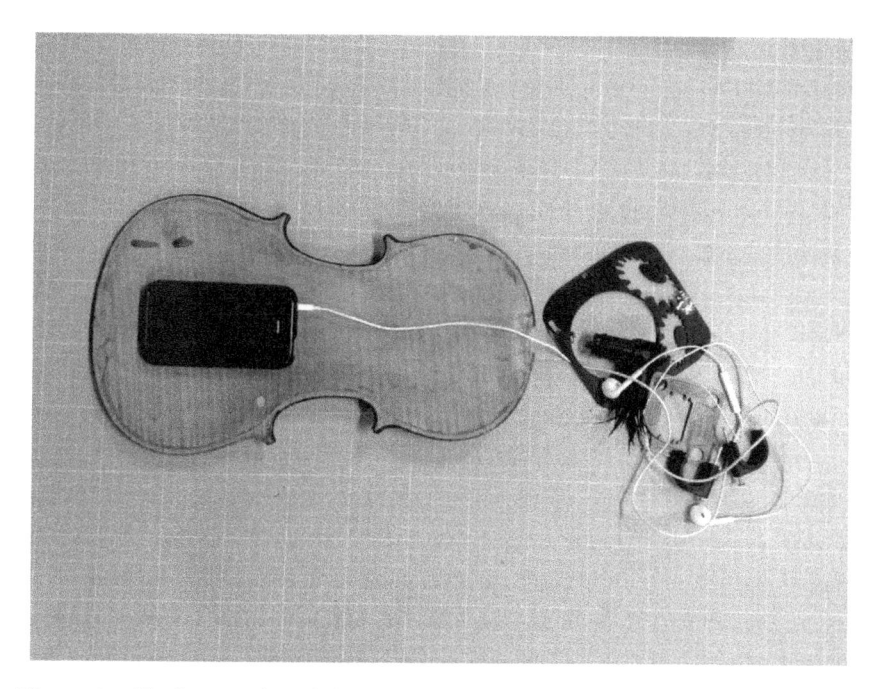

Figure 4.1 The hungry digital ghost by Tania Ivanka.

In this chapter we place the disruptive potential of uncertainty at the core of our discussion and examine its power as a generative technology. We build on the critique developed in Chapter 2, of the frequent pairing of uncertainty with risk, which defines it as something that is in need of mitigation and control. If we acknowledge uncertainty as inevitable and not something that we can avert or regulate against, then we can begin to seek ways in which to harness it for productive purposes. Simultaneously we do not deny that uncertainty is often experienced as unwelcome and can be a threatening mode of anticipation of the unknown or what has not yet happened. Indeed, uncertainty is not a tame beast. However, when we shift the terms of our engagement with uncertainty by starting from the premise that uncertainty is always present and always disruptive, this subsequently requires us to discuss how we might divert the consequences of disruption so that it can be harnessed in generative ways. This also means that when disruption is inevitable we need to seek ways to embrace its possibility and to move with it. Likewise if uncertainty is characterized by precarity, then we need to acknowledge when this precarity is destructive and find possible reroutings of this. This is not to deny that on a much wider scale, we should activate against the unethical movements or uses of power, inequalities and prejudice that lead to destructive forms of uncertainty, as part of a contemporary world. But rather that we need to learn how to recognize when and where we might divert energy towards transformative processes.

We first discuss how disruptive practices and concepts have been situated and used productively in design, anthropology and sociology. We then draw on examples of our experience of technologies (objects, methods, practices), observations and reflections of disruption as they played out in relatively 'safe' environments across our series of *Design+Ethnography+Futures* workshops. We initially reflect on how disruption was developed in more structured contexts, towards finally accounting for riskier disruptions. In doing so we both account for how disruption can be used in 'smoother' processes that lead to new ways of making and thinking, and highlight the fraught and challenging dimensions that can ensue when disruption becomes destructive. We argue that careful attention to disruption and its effects and affects enables us to create generative forms of uncertainty, which can open up the possibility to think, imagine and collaborate in workshops in ways that go beyond what is already known. However we also discuss what happens when disruption goes too far for some participants, how they have commented on this, and what we can learn from the retreats participants might make when disruption exceeds or misses its generative potential.

Contemporary (dis)alignments

Our *Design+Ethnography+Futures* research programme sought to explore and test techniques of disruption in ways that revise existing scholarly and designerly approaches. Our initial aim was to undermine the certainties that inform conventional and disciplinary ways of knowing, and challenge what we habitually thought we already did. The intention to disrupt our own ways of knowing and researching was also fuelled by the emergence of a new wave of design anthropology, led by scholars including Tim Ingold, Wendy Gunn, Jared Donovan, Rachel Charlotte Smith and Ton Otto. Disruption features strongly in design anthropology. It resists being a neat and seamless coupling and aims to 'corrupt' and break down established constructs. The anthropologists, Keith Murphy and George Marcus (2013: 261) see it as a disruptive blending to 'dismantle ethnography's ageing frame, tear it down to its most basic elements, and then reconstruct something new ... with the goal of rebuilding the core engine of anthropology'. In this iteration of design anthropology, the urge towards disruption is framed as a movement in one direction whereby anthropology as a practice might be refigured by researchers who are incorporating co-design, creative and speculative methods into their approaches. This is demonstrated to some extent in the accounts collected in the edited books on design anthropology by Gunn and Donovan (2012) and Gunn, Otto and Smith (2013), where a range of different relationships and forms of fusing between design and anthropology have been explored. The notion of disruption echoes many interdisciplinary endeavours that necessitate the abandonment of competence and specialism to

> enter a terrain beset with fears of inability, lack of expertise and the dangers of failure. The transformational experience of interdisciplinary work produces a potentially destabilising engagement with existing power structures, allowing the emergence of fragile forms of new and untested experience, knowledge and understanding. (Rendell 2013: 119)

These inter- or trans-disciplinary movements, all of which have disruptive intentions in some way or other, formed a backdrop to our work. However, our intention was also to seek to push this further, beyond the disciplinary coupling of design and anthropology, towards a more blended form of practice (e.g. Light 2015; Pink, Akama and Ferguson 2017). This in itself, both methodologically and in its aims as a form of practice, sought not to simply disrupt an existing reality that was separate from the methodology that was being applied to it. Instead we sought to disrupt ethnographic and design practice by using techniques of disruption to 'undo' some of their principles.

Our interest in modes of disruption came early in the enquiry as we discovered that it was the first step in our process of creating uncertainty.

Recognizing this, *Design+Ethnography+Futures* was interested in change by foregrounding that 'we are always working with emergent qualities and with people with whom we share journeys into the immediate future … we seek to work with ever-changing circumstances, to improvise and open up passages… . Through our research we invite people along on a journey, to together discover, question, converse and reflect on our ways of being in and understanding the world, and how we become "with" one another' (Akama, Pink and Fergusson 2015: 532–3). 'Becoming with' (borrowing from Haraway 2008) is an important aspect of our research, indicating a companionship in embarking on this endeavour and a commitment to travel along together, rather than being in fear of making 'others'. This fellow journeying is central to our approach so that disruption is enacted, explored and experienced together. Yet, as we discuss further below, disruption can always go too far, as demonstrated by instances when, although our workshops were intentional and facilitated, some participants in our more open workshops left, opted out or felt extreme discomfort that ranged from confusion to frustration.

Here, we elaborate on a tricky balance of how tight or open the structures of a workshop should be, and how much a facilitator openly shares or conceals their decisions with the participants. These questions concern how we might use uncertainty as a technology, and emphasize that as with any technology this is one that we need to learn to use, and this chapter provides examples of how such learning can come about. Some workshops provided a set of simple instructions like *Essaying the FabPod* (see Chapter 6) or *Myths of the Near Future* (this chapter) and others made the structure available for adjustment, like *Temple Works* (see Chapter 5). There is no neat script for a workshop since each emerged from the contingent circumstances of the facilitators, the theme, location and the stage of exploration that we had reached in the *Design+Ethnography+Futures* process. The number of participants, their degree of comfort with one another and the familiarity with the *Design+Ethnography+Futures* 'attitude' also mattered, thus bringing together a set of variables that shaped how a workshop balances on a knife-edge. In each workshop, the lead facilitator took responsibility and made an intuited call, often based on past experience, on the structure imposed upon a workshop and also how those structures are reconfigured, usually on the fly in response to the group's engagement. There is no 'right' way, but rather because these structures matter in the kinds of uncertainty generated, the ways in which they work requires interrogation.

Making as disruption

At our second *Design+Ethnography+Futures* workshop, we initiated a practice of inviting guest facilitators to bring a theme to the workshop, and to play this out through a series of activities developed in consultation with the organizers (Yoko and Sarah). Dèbora Lanzeni, an anthropologist of technology design and futures, and Elisenda Ardèvol, whose areas of expertise includes anthropology of design and digital cultures, led the *Spaces of Innovation* workshop in April 2014 to create forms of uncertainty that would disrupt participants' ways of thinking through exposing them to a series of increasingly structured activities concerned with seeking to connect, reshape and rehearse different ways to draw a space. The *Spaces of Innovation* workshop navigated through the conventions of design and ethnography in meandering ways. As an assemblage of practices drawn from design, makerspaces, ethnography and documentary practice, the workshop was not just one of these, but rather disrupted the ways that all of them would conventionally be practiced. It was sparked by the in-depth ethnography being undertaken by Dèbora Lanzeni in makerspaces across Barcelona and London (e.g. Lanzeni 2016), and the ways in which Lanzeni had encountered herself, among the techies who inhabit these spaces, as part of a processual world, where emergence is part of the way that things happen, and certainty is continually extended through new uses or combinations of materials, techniques or ideas. These creative spaces are driven by citizenship and institutions blossoming all around the world. Living Labs, City Labs, FabLabs, Hackerspaces, Makerspaces, co-workings, hubs and so on are the new centres where people converge to think, create, make, experience, participate and share knowledge in the cities where they dwell. This is a setting where the dynamic of creation is much more intertwined with the social everyday life, thus unfolding un-traced innovation paths. A context in which, from relations in movement, emerge new qualities that are not defined so far. These qualities could be envisioned as a space from where we might generate ideas of open futures. The workshop did not seek to reproduce the makerspace, but to invoke its qualities through a series of staged activities that participants were asked to enact and which invited generative forms of material making using playful practices with yarn, wires and mental networks (see colour Figure 4.2). The workshop was attended by more than thirty people from a range of fields including acoustics, media, architecture, business, design, anthropology and education.

The *Spaces of Innovation* workshop provided us with a set of principles that invoked the ways that Dèbora's ethnographic ways of knowing were disruptive of conventional cultural narratives about technological futures and innovation. Through the three-part structure of the workshop it sought to somehow follow these experiences and to invoke them in reduced and intensified forms. The three stages were organized following the aim to 'connect', and to reach a relational concept of space, whereby space is produced through the connections we trace. To achieve this the facilitators proposed 'building up' space together, and thus basing the workshop in the idea of *sensemaking – making sense of what we do together* which prevails within makerspaces, co-worker spaces, hackerspaces and Urban Labs where making is a central action that gives sense to what people do and how people engage with others and co-inhabit communal spaces. The activities that we programmed for the workshop were inspired by how people come together around technology making and how process of innovation and inspiration emerge in makerspaces.

The process of the workshop created an initial sense of disruption, on the basis of which two stages of generative creativity were developed. It is not our intention here to focus on the detail of exactly what happened in the workshop, but to reflect on how it moved through its different stages, how we were subsequently able to document it, and what we learnt from this mode of exploration. The first stage collectively considered what our space is like, what defines it and how we address it. This stage seemed the most confusing where we felt lost, were unsure where to go and indeed some participants left. Here the workshop began to dislodge some of the dominant rationales for why and how we do things, and disrupted the idea that we are working into structures of certainty which will have some predetermined outcomes. Using the materials that were provided, participants set about their task, with no certainty about what they were actually going to do. Threads were strung across the room, seeking connections and making loose structures, the forms of which were not certain or clear to us. By explicitly removing the predetermined outcomes, the present and future became uncertain.

The second stage sought to reshape and refine the concepts that the group had worked on in the first preview stage, thus determining what was not needed for a common notion of space. The tasks that the participants developed were more defined. They were offered more certainty in terms of the outcomes that were expected, but nevertheless the task remained open. In this stage participants drew on the resources of their own practice; we saw architects and designers beginning to create building-like structures, makers creating things that had their own logics and academics in media research beginning to work with media artefacts. Thus we learnt how people began to improvise by pulling together enough of what they already knew and felt to enable them to step forward into uncertainty. Rehearse, the last stage, was intended to perform the possibles (Halse and Boffi 2016) of the space that we now had at our disposal. In this stage, the question of what innovation spaces should be like, guided us through a more experimental experience of space-making in which the objects and processes that were made were more clearly defined, while simultaneously breaking the boundaries of what the things they touched on or resembled in some ways usually are.

The process of video recording the workshop, a form of more-than-documentation discussed in Chapter 1, brought to the fore its structure and the ways in which it initially precluded any certainties about what might happen next. Ethnographic video documentary practice has at its core an urge to 'follow the action', yet this is perhaps an inaccurate way of thinking about video recording, since following or going with the action is not simply a past-oriented activity of going behind what has already happened. Instead video documenting (like photography) is an inevitably anticipatory mode, whereby the videomaker needs to be continually engaged with not simply documenting what *is* happening, but simultaneously to be sensing what might happen next. When videoing the *Spaces of Innovation* workshop both of these techniques were disrupted: it was difficult in the first phase to know what was actually happening as participants improvised in an environment where they did not know what to hold on to, and had to invent resources with which to proceed;

and it was likewise difficult to anticipate what to 'follow' in a context where there was no obvious route of movement through the environment, because the deep sense of uncertainty about what was happening prevailed above the possibility of anticipating what was likely to happen. As the workshop activities became increasingly structured, and as the workshop process itself became underpinned by its own history, the video-making process likewise became more familiar as part of an ecology that was in its own making, and where certain forms of imagining futures, and anticipatory modes of thinking about what things could be for, were able to emerge.

The confusing and often frustrating sense that emerged from the disruption that was produced at the beginning of the workshop enabled us to collectively reshape the principles and space of engagement we inhabited. Where we started with confusion, we ended with hope, which was scaffolded on the building of a shared set of resources and experiences, which in themselves constituted the ongoingly emergent space of the workshop.

Disrupting everyday technology norms

Disruption was structured in different ways in the *Myths of the Near Future* workshop held in June 2014, led by Katherine Moline, which created both generative and destructive dimensions. Katherine is a notable artist, curator and design researcher and she brought to this workshop the accumulation of over 20 years of practice that explore social experiences mediated by technology (see Moline 2015). For our purposes here, we only focus on one activity, where she invited participants to swap their smartphones with a stranger during the workshop (see the full account of the workshop in Akama, Moline and Pink 2016). Her suggestion to swap phones aimed to disrupt the participant's relationship with their familiar, reliable and somewhat innocuous technology by turning it into a research tool to explore what this revealed about ourselves and each other. This disruptive strategy drew from Moline's research on the production of meaning as a communal event in Surrealism and experimental design (Moline 2012), and aimed to interrogate social norms and inculcated habits that were part of the ways that people used and thought about their smartphones. It was also an opportunity to reflect on the role that smartphones play in the mediation and curation of everyday life experiences, relationships, environments and activities. The immediacy of someone accessing one's phone raised questions of how we give 'permission' to strangers to have access to our personal lives, which related to concerns about the speed, quantity, proliferation and transparency of social media privacy and control. As we note in Akama, Moline and Pink (2016: 462),

> We were interested less in the social science concern with what people (think they) usually do, to instead explore what was made possible when they let go of the fundamental assumptions that frame what they do. This refers not only to assumptions that are articulated verbally, but to tacit ways of knowing and doing that may not often be spoken about.

Disruptive research explorations to interrogate everyday habitual activities such as our relationship and use of a smartphone may not feel comfortable and can even generate resistance. The phone swapping activity deliberately disrupted social conventions. Even when Katherine explained clearly and carefully that this collaborative exploration was to interrogate these very norms and social habits, this went too far for some participants who were extremely discomforted and took up the invitation to opt out of the phone swapping activity, and instead self-reported how they use their phone. Such discomfort derived from mismatched expectations between what they thought they were led to believe before arriving and what they were invited to participate in during the workshop, which had made them feel misled by the organizers. Other participants echoed such feelings of disorientation and confusion in their feedback: 'Our table felt some discomfort in that "openness"', leading some to ask for 'additional guidance about the purposes of that experimental making as a way of knowing more how to act, how to begin, what to do.' Others reflected on the uncertainty of sharing 'unfiltered and un-staged information … it felt as a much more risky act – not because of risk of harassment. But because of feeling of sharing a chaotic unknown – without the effort of shaping or curating it for communication.' Another commented,

> Giving access to private digital data gave a sense of uncertainty and lost control. As the mobile phone is a 'thing' that assembles a lot of activities in my life, that both serves as a tool for organising – and for disorganising – I became a bit uncertain of my use of it. And to be quite frank – I had no idea of how little I know of what kind of traces I have left on the phone.

Uncertainty was a significant feature through such routes of disruption, as shared by another participant, 'Leaving an analysis of my phone's meanings and use to someone else was filled with uncertainty – uncertainty about what they might find, how they would look, what it would mean to them'.

It is interesting to note how the participants developed a range of different strategies through which to cope with the activity while working with uncertainties of the workshop, as discussed elsewhere, which involved generating new ways of protecting their privacy, by making agreements with each other about what to view, or not, or, as noted above, opting out. Many participants negotiated 'different boundaries (go and no go zones)' and improvised creatively. Whether or not participants undertook the activity as intended by the facilitator and organizers is perhaps not as significant as the disruptive act of inviting the participants to transgress the norms of privacy that they would usually adhere to, and in doing so, to interrogate their feelings and limitations. It also highlights that certain forms of willingness, as well as techniques that are required when people are invited to surrender to collective activities that involve stepping into an uncertain territory. In this case participants were asked to exceed limits that were deeply personal, given that they involved sharing what was usually private. In the next chapter we extend this discussion of personal and collective surrender further through a demonstration of how it might be played out successfully in a rather and more encompassing sensory and experiential environment.

The technique of disruption in this workshop had two further benefits (Akama, Moline and Pink 2016). One was part of the structure of the workshop in that it led on to the second stage where participants were asked to disrupt the image-making algorithm of their smartphones by creating images from materials supplied that differed from their usual photographs (Figure 4.1). In this sense the phase of disruption served to open up the possibilities that communications technologies and the rules around their uses might be different, and to invite participants to take this further. This process echoed the maker logics that had been explored in the previous *Spaces of Innovation* workshop discussed above, however this was more structured since the objectives of making were more thematic, thus offering participants a firmer base from which to improvise, and thus to generate new modes of knowing and experiencing. The second benefit of this process was to generate thematic insights of interest to the field of mobile media studies and privacy, since, by asking participants to exceed the boundaries of the way they already knew and understood privacy, the exercise revealed new modes through which these could be navigated. As existing research across a range of different cultural, national and religious contexts has shown (see for example Pink, Horst et al. 2016; Waltrop 2017) mobile and smartphone privacy and/or sharing access is conceptualized and navigated in different ways across different circumstances and with a range of different effects. In this sense the workshop did not offer definitive findings on this topic but rather revealed how the forms of disruption and awareness that were associated with uncertainty enabled participants to both reveal their concerns and improvise into a new scenario.

The video documentation process of the *Myths of the Near Future* workshop was much different to that of the *Spaces of Innovation* workshop. Because uncertainty was more explicit, shocking and verbalized by participants, it created more surface activities that brought people together in action in groups that could be filmed as they entered into open-ended discussions and making activities (see colour Figure 3.4). Here, the video-making process could follow a story, or pick up on the feelings or activities that grew out of the processes of sharing smartphone contents. However, the activities themselves also disrupted the video process, since the contents of the phones were also not something that would normally be revealed in such an open way in video ethnography. For example, in recent video ethnography projects where smartphone screens have been shown, participants have been invited to consider carefully what they would be happy to show and what not to show, including questions of anonymity where relevant. These options were likewise open to participants in the workshop, meaning that the video-making process was similarly contingent on a new layer of decisions beyond those relating to participation in the workshop activity, which could, through non-participation, in turn disrupt the process of video recording and in doing so the workshop process itself. Thus, as we see processes of disruption, far from being controlled by workshop facilitators, can fold in on themselves.

Myths of the Near Future therefore developed a series of insights into how uncertainty can generate multiple forms of improvisation within the same workshop site.

Structuring tension and balance

When we embarked on the series of *Design+Ethnography+Futures* workshops, one of the challenges was to investigate how to facilitate exploration, not with regard to what we already knew, but in relation to what we did not yet know. This required a form of disruption on the part of the instigators including Sarah, Yoko and the guest facilitator of each workshop. This was an uncharted territory as we trod a narrow path between chaos and control, and most importantly tried to avoid making the participants feel like a subject of novel experiments with little value in return. In the examples discussed above, we have accounted for two workshops where the majority of the participants felt able to work and engage with the structure of a process. We now account for the final event in our series of workshops where we placed uncertainty at the very centre of the structure and design of an event, and in doing so pushed it further towards its limits. This process both enabled Sarah and Yoko, with the participants, to create generative forms of uncertainty through disruption, but at the same time revealed moments where participants' feelings of being unsettled caused them to retreat back to the sites of their practice where they already felt comfortable, and to articulate the ways in which they found these experiences problematic. Through this we learnt both about the affects and effects of uncertainty as a process, as well as gaining new insights into the limits of interdisciplinarity.

Simple oblique strategies were trialled from the beginning of the *Design+Ethnography+Futures* series. These included not introducing who we were at the start of the workshop, letting participants get to know each other by simply forming their own groups and embarking on an activity together. We had learnt earlier on that sharing someone's professional positions inhibited engagement, for example setting hierarchies between a student and a professor or reproducing professional seniority. Self-introductions that can often reveal job titles was therefore avoided. This practice continued into the two-day *Un/certainty* symposium held in December 2014 that invited twenty-eight participants. The aim of this symposium was to propose an event that pushed away from the closed, objectified and more certain stances through which knowledge is presented and discussed. This was also coherent with a turn against the symposium as a site for communicating knowledge objects towards it as a process for experiencing and generating uncertainty as the very theme of the gathering. The symposium was documented through images, texts and videos. Many artefacts were created as part of the process: video vox-pops, group performances, a meal and, ultimately, the digital, self-published *Un/certainty* ebook from which much of the reporting in this chapter comes. In such instances, quotes will appear as 'in Un/certainty' and we welcome readers to browse through the ebook to experience its media-rich composition in complement to this chapter.

Acknowledging that the participants were senior and notable academics in design, anthropology and creative practice, the organizers did not circulate biographies prior to their gathering but asked for 'invocations' as a way of introductions of each other. The request for *invocations* also had the double disruptive intention of contesting the convention of requesting summative abstracts or joust-like provocations that are commonly shared before an academic conference. Instead it called on participants to contribute through a different mode through which to engage others. The lay meaning of 'invoke' is to call on for earnest desire; make supplication or pray for; to declare something; to appeal to; call on for help or aid; to bring about (www.dictionary.com). It was chosen because of its tricky definition in an academic context and to set the stage for unknown and uncertain encounters. However it was also intended to be an invitation to connect. Questions were sent to the delegates through e-mail: 'How do you invoke uncertainty? How do you encounter and confront uncertainty in your work?' The organizers also asked the invitees to 'think about how you would like to creatively engage with uncertainty. This may be in regard to a specific practice with which you engage or it may be a more general or personal invocation to uncertainty' (pers. comm. 31 July 2014). In response to this invitation, Martin Berg, a Swedish scholar in sociology, expressed how this request led to a disorienting experience as well as a will to explore it;

> it struck me that I had no idea of what an academic invocation was, how it should look, feel or sound. It should not be an abstract, nor should it be a provocation. So what should it be then? I began questioning the task as such, thinking that this was actually a clever move by the organizers to make me encounter and confront uncertainty already at this stage. I was impressed and started thinking about my work in relation to the question of uncertainty. (*Un/certainty* 2015: 17)

The invocations are a collection of musings, a list, a poem, an image or a statement ranging from inspirations to interrogations (see http://d-e-futures.com/events/uncertainty-symposium/) that indicates that many had embraced an oblique request and became a rich starting point for the symposium and a tone that ebbed in and out through the two days.

Such requests by the organizers reflected their attempt to prepare what the participants might expect from this symposium, which was communicated personally via e-mail, phone or in person. Conventional structures were dismantled and explained to ensure uncertainty was not imposed or taken for granted, even for a symposium centred on the theme of uncertainty with academics who were invited based on their willingness to encounter and explore uncertainty together. Yet several participants remarked on needing more to be explained prior to their attendance, including the purpose, benefits and outcomes of attending a symposium. Such questions are commonly asked by academics who are often time-poor and required to account for their days away from their offices as contributions in productive, measurable terms. Here marks the dilemma of placing uncertainty in conventional contexts and how expectations are attended to or not, which is compelling to examine for the purpose of this chapter. The following accounts were pieced together from correspondences between several participants and Yoko to critically reflect on how disruption was structured and experienced.

Tension between looseness and tightness, experimentation and predictability, chance and expectation accompanied the two full days of the symposium that were sometimes voiced as frustration and other times sensed as enjoyment, both in extreme ways. The assembled academics were also sensitive to and articulate about power differentials. This combination made them eager to join in and contribute critical questions, and this high degree of critique was put to one another and to the organizers during and after the event. To demonstrate this we take a slice through one pair of activities on Day 1 – a lunch-making exercise and its reflective discussion afterwards. This marks out the extreme contrasts between both a conventional symposium and the uncertainty symposium and between traditional boundaries between design and ethnography that speaks to uncertainty and its disruptive qualities. The lunch-making activity was organized by dividing the attendees into two groups, the makers and observers. The makers were asked to create a meal from the ingredients and resources supplied, and the observers were asked to document the process of making with materials they had to hand. The dishes had to be created according to colour categories and within an hour. This structure and instruction might seem simple and straightforward, yet it had two contrasting qualities. The first account speaks of its generative dimension, the second account speaks to its destructive features. In doing so, we aim to shed a light on its inherent uncertainty, and how, why and where it teetered on a knife-edge and swayed it one way or another for different participants.

Disruption as a generative catalyst: the lunch-making task

The maker group, largely composed of researchers who were known for their ethnographic practice, were provided with a constrained brief – to make a meal for everyone only using the resources available (kitchen with a gas cooker and microwave) and with the variety of fresh and colourful ingredients purchased that morning at the nearby farmer's market and made available to them. In addition to this more mundane preparation task, there was a playful emphasis that the meal should be colourful. The timing of the exercise around 1pm meant that everyone was peckish or hungry, so it could be said that the makers had no choice. Their only means of eating was to cook the meals together. However, it was notable that no one complained about this restriction or elected to go to the café downstairs. Rather the makers threw themselves into the tasks allocated and formed 'colour tables', willingly improvising within the constraints and affordances of the ingredients, resources of the workshop venue and collective teamwork (see colour Figures 4.3, 4.4 and 4.5). Many exhibited adventurous and playful combinations that risked being inedible or joked about the mixtures raising potential health issues, reflected in accounts like, 'What is it? It might give us a tummy ache' or 'What is that? [smelling] … It might need to be cooked …? That's very uncertain' (in *Un/certainty* 2015: 25–31). The makers were thus implicated in the process and outcome, bringing a heightened level of care and obligation towards this exercise as they lived it out in authentic and performative ways. Frequent tasting, smelling, feeling the ingredients before and during the making, and constant consultation and feedback among different groups (including makers and observers) were witnessed. This resulted in tables of red, green and brown that wonderfully combined a visual and delicious feast.

Eating, one of the most fundamental human acts and inherently oriented to sharing, was conducive to breaking the ice among teams that deliberately grouped strangers together. In this sense, it did not seem that important to know who each other were and what level of disciplinary academic expertise each possessed, rather, the focus was on the pragmatics of drawing upon their practices of everyday cooking and living. We note how the lunch-making experience shared characteristics of practices, of making do with what's available and working with hunches or tacit senses, even when the scripts are tight and expectations are uncertain. No one simply followed a recipe, which they could have done by looking on the internet, but rather invented things presented by the situation or ideating opportunities. Run-of-the-mill dishes were abandoned in favour of more unusual and challenging dishes. We can see this in a remark about the pregnant-cucumber-dish by Soile Veijola: 'The idea is not mine ... it's the gentleman in pink ... perhaps we might do something [carving the cucumber] ... its twins! [placing gherkins inside the cucumber]' (ibid.: 29). Elaborate techniques were spontaneously invented, such as sheets of paper wrapped as cones to work as a piping tube to artistically display a '... shies and rocket mousse ... to cover the crackers completely' (ibid.: 30). One of the most memorable dishes was presented by Martin Berg's team: 'Because we are very passionate so we have a passion-guacamole, which resembles how we feel about this fantastic exercise' (ibid.: 30). This dip was remarked by many as the most unexpected, delicious dish that combined the unconventional pairing of passion fruit and avocado. This indicates how many surrendered to the flow of random ideas inspired by the colour theme that gave birth to unusual dishes previously unthought-of, as well as a surrendering to one another and other things in the movement of making (we discuss surrender further in Chapter. 5).

It is clear to see that conventional markers became mutable and malleable so that the makers moved beyond them: 'Here, we sensed a commitment to uncertainty as the makers explored in various ways; through tasting unusual ingredients, by combining them in experimental ways; by trusting the hunch of their fellow team members; by inventing techniques of cooking and preparing' (in *Un/certainty* 2015: 33). While the activities preceding this lunch-making exercise asked participants to share and locate uncertainty analytically, reflectively in reference to their research, the lunch experience provided insights to how each performed in uncertainty. By disrupting conventional approaches to making food and eating at symposia, new collaborations and imaginaries were constituted. This means that uncertainty as technology manifested in the dishes, in the actions, in the methods, created and improvised in situ by drawing upon past practices and current resources. In other words, it was a technology of knowing about oneself in relation to others in raw and unfiltered ways.

Disruption as a destructive force: ethnographies of lunch

Nevertheless, not all of the outcomes of this disruptive exercise were experienced as positive. The division of teams placed too blunt a distinction between the maker and observer groups. Most of the anthropologists were grouped as makers and the creative researchers (including designers) were placed in the observer group by the organizers as a way to reverse roles and organize against type. However, this inadvertently made the disciplinary boundaries literal and arbitrary. This frustrated those who practiced both design and ethnography and diminished the possibility for an expansive experience. Furthermore, while the maker group were given productive constraints, the observer group were given very little to go on, other than to document the making and tasting experiences with the materials they had to hand. While a few saw this to be an invitation to experiment with audio, video and visual recordings through their smartphones, and some became tasters to give feedback to the many dishes during its preparation (see colour Figure 4.5), for others, this lack of instruction and structure was interpreted as a lack of need and value and provided little camaraderie for their contributions. In comparison to the emphasis given to the maker group who were performing and producing amazing dishes in teams, some observers felt they were isolated individuals with little expectation for their outcomes and minimal group momentum or commonality to bond with one another. We can acknowledge how this would make participants feel peripheral to the exercise, and one participant candidly shared later how this did indeed result in a frustrating, disappointing and boring experience. Additionally, for the anthropologists in the group, the experience of documenting or undertaking mini-ethnographies of the food-making activity was compromised by their disciplinary expectations, in which research would need to be more immersive, longer term and implicated. The contrast between the maker and observer groups are extreme when we compare the structures for uncertainty that can create or inhibit generative possibilities. It made us aware the extent to which uncertainty can be situated in the instructions, directiveness, method or outcomes of an exercise. The ones who did best had clear instructions and a sense of purpose, an open-ended method and only the broadest stipulation of outcome: something for everyone to eat. They embraced the opportunity to work in groups and make colourful creations. The observers, by contrast, had less instruction and their uncertainty lay in what to do in relation to what others were doing. The need for creativity sat in a different relationship with the exercise. It is also worth observing that at other points in the same workshop, those less engaged participants found joyful activities which they performed collaboratively with even less structure. But the exercise here served to draw attention to the impact of uncertainty in different parts of the generative process.

Reflecting on the lunchtime exercise further exacerbated divisions between the makers and observers, which was already at a rift. Perhaps the act of reflection, analysis and synthesis necessitated some to use traditional framings of disciplines – in this case anthropology – to interrogate what had occurred. This interrogation by anthropologists was at the centre of the ensuing discussion of the activity, and brought to the fore their discomfort with the exercise. This dominated the entire discussion, as Sarah and Yoko (in *Un/certainty* 2015: 34) later reflected:

> Anthropologists and ethnographers noted that they were uncertain about the process of documenting the lunch making process and found the exercise problematic and contrary to some of the principles ... of what good ethnography should mean, that it should be systematic and more embedded, not just fluttering around the edges, taking a second guess as to what to record. The almost 'hit and run' nature of the lunchtime documentation ventured too far for some for whom ethnographic practice requires more immersion, incremental ways of learning and knowing about others and understandings that are rooted in closer relationships and self-reflexive interrogations.

This echoes the lack of structure given to or created by the observer group, mentioned before, but also alludes to anthropology as a discipline that requires structure to give the work integrity and rigour. This structure is methodological, produced through an ongoing process of embedding oneself, learning and piecing together the jigsaw of what is going on in contexts which are always uncertain but where understandings grow as more solid ground begins to form under the researcher's feet. For many who spoke of uncertainty as a central condition in their research, the removal, dismantling or blatant omission of a process of building confidence and knowing structures appeared to be too precarious, producing the opposite effect to being generative. The defensive resistance that calls on 'principles' of 'good ethnography' and what it 'should be' are signs of holding on to some important certainties.

What we learn from this account is how intention, process and outcomes do not align neatly and can create uncomfortable and precarious conditions, especially when the very structures we know and rely upon are readily questioned and critiqued on the fly. A large group (twenty-eight participants) of academics is also encumbered by stronger forces in group dynamic, compared to a smaller group (under twelve participants in *Essaying the FabPod* and *Temple Works* workshops) that can be more attentive to the individuals within the group. While this might be rather obvious in hindsight, this was particularly notable for the organizers, who were also travelling alongside the participants to explore uncertain approaches to change-making, yet were also held accountable for the outcomes that ensued. One participant called this a 'tyranny of uncertainty' when structures are taken away too naively, forcefully and suddenly. We could even say that this is the problematic and unfruitful dimension of surrender, when done through force. The result was a form of disempowerment which had not been observed during the earlier *Design+Ethnography+Futures* workshops. We comment on it here as an example of how experimenting with uncertainty can lead to forms of disengagement. We also note this in relation to the theme of disciplinary boundaries, since a second learning from this exercise was that, however prepared participants were to collaborate in an interdisciplinary context, many of them – when confronted with the challenging activity – found their strength in recourse to their home discipline. It is not the kind of surrender we observed in the workshops and speak to in the other chapters, and thus helps to remind what side of disruption we ought to commit to when accompanying a journey of uncertainty.

This activity demonstrated how generative and destructive kinds of uncertainty emerge in specific moments and contexts, often unexpectedly. It reminds us that the balance between structure and an open format, which one participant pointed out in correspondence with Yoko later, should have leaned more towards structure and needed to be fine-tuned, while also revealing the insights that can be found when it is not. Ultimately this leads us to an ethical dilemma regarding the extent to which participants should be unsettled and suggests the relevance of seeking to embed some controls regarding this in processes through which uncertainty is engaged. In the next chapter, we take this question further through a focus on how feelings of being uncertain were navigated and negotiated by a small group who embarked on a collective experience that required them to surrender to uncertainty.

Considering uncertainty through disruption

In this chapter we have examined how, as a technology for disruption, forms of uncertainty can be both destructive and generative. As explained at the beginning of this book, our aim has been to demonstrate, by way of examples, how uncertainty might be engaged as a technology that intervenes to generate new forms of possibility. The examples discussed in this chapter were not always successful or manifest in the same ways for all participants. However participants' resistance, discomfort and disengagement were nevertheless valuable in learning about both uncertainty and its disruptive effects and affects. Significantly we were also, in all three workshops, able to learn about the themes that underpinned the workshops: making and futures; smartphones and privacy; and challenges of interdisciplinarity.

In this sense we offer readers two sets of insights based on the exploration in this chapter. First regarding the use of uncertainty as a technology for disruption, we argue that forms of uncertainty serve well as technologies for enabling people to reflect and improvise beyond what they already do and think they know. Yet we emphasize that every case of implementation is contingent upon many forces and factors that require a mindful and reflexive approach. As our different examples have shown, participants willingly engaged with our processes with curiosity and a collaborative approach. The first two workshops discussed here – *Spaces of Innovation* and *Myths of the Near Future* – were open to anyone, in other words people self-selected to join. The *Un/certainty* symposium was by invitation only. Thus in the symposium we sought to explore disruption further and also found our strongest critics. We had chosen our critics, rather than invited participation from a broad and curious pool of playful collaborators (though, of course, these two groups overlapped). And these participants were indeed ideally equipped to critique, given their disciplinary backgrounds as ethnographers, designers and creative research practitioners. Through their invaluable comments we were able to learn much about a precarious process, as well as about the difficulties of discipline crossing. When we pursue a methodology that puts uncertainty at its centre, we need to engage with the possibility of criticism and to take this as a basis for learning about what might be generated by uncertainty and about the questions that we seek to address through the process of making uncertain. The symposium also demonstrated how disruption was experienced very differently by workshop participants, and that it was possible for it to begin to work against the generative potential of uncertainty by shutting down engagement and frustrating imagination. Even so, while disruptive uncertainty was negatively experienced by some in the workshop setting, the critique, reflection and collective insight it subsequently enabled allowed valuable new insights to be reached by both participants and conveners. Thus the impact and ultimate value of disruption came at different times for different people, but was ultimately generative of new ways of thinking about uncertainty and change-making.

5

Surrendering to and Tracing Uncertainty

Tom Jackson, Yoko Akama, Sarah Pink and Shanti Sumartojo

Figure 5.1 The entrance to the undercroft. Photo by Tom Jackson.

In this chapter we continue our discussion of uncertainty as a technology through an exploration of how it entails a productive form of surrender. We see surrender, like disruption, as an element of uncertainty, but one that needs to be considered, drawn out and engaged with, rather than being an inevitable or careless happenstance. Indeed, also like disruption, surrender and uncertainty are co-constituting in many ways. As this book argues, we then need to explore and examine each of these attentively to consider how they can enable processual modes of change-making. As we have already emphasized with reference to disruption, change requires a great deal of effort, labour and resources – it is hard work. Building on this and with particular relevance for the theme of surrender, to achieve intentional and collective change, we may need to let go of many things like power, control, expectations, habits and entrenched ways of thinking and doing. Change, from this perspective involves a form of learning through *unlearning* (Varela et al. 1993), not by acquisition of new information but through questioning what we are already doing and know about. This chapter pursues the process and outcomes of disruptions, and in doing so, interrogates how surrender might be part of, as well as emergent from, uncertainty as a technology.

The discussion here also reiterates the need for a re-framing in order to recast uncertainty as a generative technology. This re-framing departs from negative and risk-adverse interpretations of uncertainty, as discussed in Chapter 2. It moreover re-frames surrender, not as a forceful way to subject humans and non-humans to submissive and demeaning conditions, but to see surrender as a voluntary willingness to unseat one's own certainties and begin to interrogate what is taken for granted. We see the value of surrender as a form of readiness or rehearsal for change-making to build our capacity to be fluid and fluent, to avoid knee-jerk or seemingly automated forms of defensiveness and self-preservation. There are of course contexts and situations where surrender is possible and appropriate, and those where it is not. This then becomes an exploration of how and where surrender is an ethical stance, and how interventions towards surrender might be structured in ways that are collaborative, consensual and ethical. Such careful negotiations among a group are witnessed in this chapter.

A second theme of this chapter is an erosion of oppositional categories and a willingness to embrace incomplete yet exquisite experiences as generative qualities of uncertainty. As we will see, there were heightened poles of apparent opposites between highly personal yet collective encounters where it is hard to distinguish where one starts and the other begins. Contradictory emotions also collapse, such as frustration and intrigue, as well as what is real and not real. Anxiety-fuelled imagination is felt more viscerally than what factually surrounds the explorers. Misapprehension and misinterpretation, which are usually often avoided, are embraced willingly, transfiguring another kind of rendering.

To demonstrate how various dimensions of surrender can play out in practice, we develop a narrative from twelve participants who were willing and prepared to be made uncertain. We account for the discoveries that they collectively made through their surrender to the conditions, circumstances, environment and to one another, through their participation in the *Temple Works* workshop. For the purposes of this chapter's discussion, co-authors Yoko Akama and Tom Jackson who facilitated the workshop and took part in it, layer their reflective rendition together with what was shared by the participants. In doing so, the chapter foregrounds various dimensions of disruption, surrender and moving beyond that relate to risk and openness and that help to progress our thoughts on uncertainty as technology. Several traces of how uncertainty was experienced are discussed in the section below. They are indicated as passages taken from the self-published *Temple Works* online book (available at https://issuu.com/templeworks/docs/temple_works_2015 and cited here as *Temple Works* 2015) that was designed and curated through what the group made together. Yoko and Tom begin the following story from the time of arrival and how the participants prepared to step into uncertainty at *Temple Works*.

Preparing

Temple Works is shrouded in myth and mystery, chosen by the organizers for this very reason to explore uncertainty. It is a Grade I listed building in Holbeck, in the centre of Leeds, UK, built as a flax mill by John Marshall who played a key role in establishing the Leeds flax industry in 1938. Its mysterious aura emanates from its very architecture, designed by Joseph and Ignatius Bonomi, who gave homage to the origins of flax by modelling its façade on an Egyptian temple, Horus at Edfu (Figure 5.2). Many myths are told in stories of its roof that was apparently grassed and mowed by a flock of sheep, and rumours of resident ghosts of former workers and people who got lost, perhaps perishing in a space underneath the building called the 'undercroft'.

All eleven workshop participants gathered at *Temple Works* on 22 June 2015 and remarked on this exterior of a building that stood out ominously among dark, rain-pregnant clouds, setting the mood, igniting curiosity and heightening anticipation for what they might encounter there. One of the participants, Rachel Clarke shared: 'What was this place? It looked more like a masonic lodge than a flax mill and it was behind bars' (in *Temple Works* 2015: 22).

Figure 5.2 A building with many myths and a mysterious aura. Photo by Rachel Clarke.

Alex McLean and Erinma Ochu described, 'Arriving, late and lost and apprehensive about what was on the other side of the door' (ibid.: 63). Tom Jackson, a co-facilitator of this workshop, reflected, 'I felt uncertain that the unconventional format and location would be well received' (ibid.: 47). Here, we can see that uncertainty was already emerging as an affordance of this space as well as in the thoughts of the people assembling, like the rain-clouds that shrouded the sky upon arrival. These 'anticipatory affects' (Sumartojo 2014: 61) were carried within the participants to this site of gathering, contributing to the atmosphere of the workshop. There was already a heightened sense of disorienting and disquiet, thus introducing different forms of disruption, even before the workshop began.

Different kinds of preparatory states emerged in this context in the face of the prospect of stepping into uncertain encounters, and can be glimpsed here. One form of preparedness can be seen in contingency measures that participants developed, consciously or unconsciously in order to minimize risk and negative consequences of uncertainty. As discussed in Chapter 2, such ways of mitigating risk are culturally embedded in the ways of life of many (but not necessarily all) parts of the world. In this workshop example, contingency measures for uncertainty were observed by participants who brought a map to avoid getting lost when locating the workshop and raincoats and umbrellas for the inclement weather. The hard hats that were worn when Susan Williamson (former director of the Temple.Works.Leeds creative and cultural project) guided the participants around the two-acre building represent another kind of preparedness in the form of the Occupational Safety and Health measures that are typical of anticipatory logics, audit cultures and the regulatory regimes of neoliberal societies (Pink, Morgan and Dainty 2015). As the group walked through a rapidly deteriorating building where some parts were under threat of collapse through age, weathering and architectural flaws from the time of construction, Yoko wrote, 'We were instructed not to stand under, next to, or on top of specific parts of the building, and the crumbling, rusting, collapsing structure was visible to our unqualified eye … the paint peels like sunburnt skin and the patchwork mold … decorates the brickwork' (Akama in *Temple Works* 2015: 7).

Another form of preparedness, different to minimizing risk, but still a way of 'managing' uncertainty, is seen in equipment (or technology) brought along by participants – pens, notebooks, cameras, microphones, recording devices, butchers paper, sticky tape and various drawing implements. The materials brought here, ready to hand, represent many options, potential and possibility rather than imbuing an execution plan. Indeed this readiness in the participants' states and in the materials they brought can be understood as significant accompaniments to stepping into uncertainty. In this sense we can see them as bringing with them things and processes that were familiar, as a means through which to anticipate how they might step into the unknown, and as a way of creating continuities between what they might have done in already known circumstances and what they might do in uncertain ones. In this sense their improvisatory actions were always both rooted in and departing from the familiar, as actions that took as their launch pad a base of sufficient confidence to be able to move forward, while acknowledging elements of the unknown. Taken together, this echoes the kinds of materials, readiness and approaches in co-design that facilitators bring as a way to access latent creativity of ordinary people (Sanders 2002) and co-create representations and scenarios with participants to prototype possible futures (Halse 2013).

As the examples discussed in the previous chapter have already shown, disruption and surrender are necessary stages to step into uncertainty and its generative potential, but these stages also require slow and gentle manoeuvring to make sure it is not forced upon the participants. Yet in this workshop, disruption was already part of the participants' disorientation and discomfort upon arrival, due to conditions and stories of the building. Tom observed how people huddled together, 'seeking the familiarity and reassurance associated with those relationships' (Jackson in *Temple Works* 2015: 47), noticed through his time-lapse video. Its temporal compression of 10 minutes into 27 seconds shows bodies that cluster and morph in different ways, 'allowing relationships to be more easily identified' (ibid.). In order to reorientate the destructive feelings the participants were reassured at the beginning by a warming cup of tea and coffee, a welcome and an introduction by Susan, Tom and Yoko.

During this introduction, preparing was suggested by co-facilitator Yoko Akama, as one of the stages to be undertaken during the first thirty minutes of the workshop.

> I suggest a rough road-map for the day – the idea of four moves – preparing, sensing, capturing and sharing uncertainty. In clusters of small groups, preparing involves murmurs of conversations. Some are brainstorming words on paper. … I hear evocative snippets in others; 'giving over agency …', 'permission …', 'rehearsing to be open …', 'sensory is selective …', 'the sensing and action is coupled, not passive …', 'leave distractions behind …' (Akama in *Temple Works* 2015: 7)

These snippets of eavesdropping might suggest how participants were readying to surrender agency, control and of the sensory, giving hints to various ways participants were readying for an uncertain encounter. This stage of preparing for uncertainty – in acknowledging discomfort, taking the time for people to find reassurance in each other and share their feelings and thoughts – seems to have emboldened the group to undertake activities that could be considered high-risk. Just as with the discussion of attunement in Chapter 6, participants were considering how to attend to the detail of their anticipated experience of the *Temple Works* site and the particular affects and thoughts it might engender. This gradual process of surrender – to the risky and mysterious site, to the coming experience in and of it and to the structure of the workshop format – mirrored their entry into the structure and the exploration of it that was yet to come.

Locating uncertainty

Children and families of the flax mill lived in the space underneath the building that Susan called the 'undercroft', and she explained that there were dormitories, shops, doctors and a church – a whole community of workers under the auspices of the industrialist, John Marshall. During the guided tour, the undercroft was explicitly indicated as a no-go zone for the participants to enter. There were rumours of people getting lost due to its labyrinthine passages. Several participants attribute this ominous warning as the very ignition to explore this space, almost like a dare. After the guided tour and a hasty discussion, the group decided to form a human chain to descend into total darkness (Figure 5.1) – a clever suggestion by one of the participants. This suggestion accommodated ways to mitigate any risk of getting lost, while allowing the group to viscerally experience how it felt like to explore the space. The person on one end could keep a view of the exit in their periphery, and the person on the other end could go as far as the human chain could extend.

In undertaking this exploration, some participants were more willing whereas some were hesitant, even anxious, and these degrees of emotion seemed to dictate the positioning on the human chain. Simon Bowen indicated the greatest willingness by self-electing to be the leader of the human chain.

> Simon walks in without another thought, reaching out his hand and saying 'I need a hand, somebody' and equally impulsively, I take it and become his shadow, or as we get darker, his comrade at the front of the pack, trusting and intrepid, with no hands of my own, one being possessed by him and the other grabbed by the next in the chain … Simon and me, as the vanguard, had pushed on slowly, turning a wall and stopping, pulling everyone out of the lit zone and making the experiment count. (Light in *Temple Works* 2015: 53)

As this bizarre collaboration of sorts progressed further and further down the passages in progressive darkness, many noticed how other senses and emotions start to capture the experience. 'Discomfort turns into adventure, emboldened by each other's touch, voices and closeness. I feel the uneven surfaces with my feet and notice a musty draft on my face. Simon at the lead shouts out that there's something above, so watch out. Oh my god' (Akama in *Temple Works* 2015: 8). A verbal caution, sharp intake of breath, a tug in another direction, a tightening grip – these stimuli experienced through various sensory modalities are shared among the participants, representing a wealth of 'information' about our responses to the environment. Similarly, warnings, physical obstacles and sensory observations were helpfully passed down the chain, but these seem to have heightened further imagination and anxiety for some. The draft felt by one person is shared and interpreted by another as wing-flaps because he is ornithophobic. Edgar Gomez Cruz writes, 'What if this is their headquarters? Can pigeons live in the dark? Wait ... bats can do that. What if there are bats here that will be confused with pigeons? A wing is a wing after all. What would happen if we accidentally step on a nest?' (Gomez Cruz in *Temple Works* 2015: 35). Other forms of imaginations induce other anxieties: 'It seems massive and cavernous, and I imagine stalactites, bats and pools of dank water where eye-less amphibians dwell. Did Susan say there was a resident ghost?' (Akama in *Temple Works* 2015: 8). Uncertainty here worked powerfully to generate imaginative responses to the undercroft space that filled in possibilities beyond the limits of sensory perception, acting as one example of 'objects and practices that bring about imaginative effects' (Sneath, Holbraad and Pedersen 2009: 20), making available new ways of thinking that 'are nevertheless essentially unpredictable and often unintended' (ibid.: 22).

Despite the collaborative nature of the exploratory human-chain snaking into the *Temple Works* undercroft, it was comprised of many individuals, each of whom encountered the space in particular ways. Uncertainty featured differently as highly individualized experiences while the activity was undertaken collectively. The written reflections produced after the event described a range of personal accounts that give different reasons to why this exercise became the most memorable. This was an immutable phobia for Edgar Gomez Cruz; situated knowledge for Tom Jackson; familiarity with other participants for Ann Light; and sense memories for Helen Thornham. We notice this echoing the 'Rashomon Effect' (Anderson 2016) of contrasting interpretations of the same event. This reveals another productive site for exploring uncertainty as moments when shared experiences distinctly converge or diverge in their reception. These moments reveal the impossibility in attempting to achieve a 'singular truth' of an event and also how generative potential might come from embracing heterogeneous and conflicting stories. Darkness seems to have been the strongest contributing factor to our experiences of uncertainty, interwoven with sensations that are hard to pinpoint, fuelling unpleasant imaginations. When someone suggests they light up their phone to look at where they are, several share their disappointment; 'there we are in a dank space full of brick and breezeblock with a rough concrete floor beneath us but no mystery' (Light in *Temple Works* 2015: 53). Photographs taken in this space show spray paint on the wall with an original slogan, 'IAN WAS HERE' and discarded rubbish – 'an empty Quakers packet on the floor' (Akama in *Temple Works* 2015: 8). Such traces indicate how many must have ventured in the undercroft space before (since the mill workers) and their implied flippancy towards this environment, indicated by the graffiti and rubbish, stands out as jarring with our unique experience. 'When we turn on our lights in a moment of reveal, to disrupt the experience and make known the otherwise unknown, it was already known. There was a flag, a marker and an echo of a past presence that made us repetitive. I think we were the iterations' (Thornham in *Temple Works* 2015: 67). When the uncertainty regarding their physical surroundings was removed by the illumination of the space, all of their imaginations were replaced by a far more prosaic reality. Their accounts suggest a disappointing reveal but it becomes apparent that this had not detracted from the earlier experience. In fact, not only had the exhilaration of sensing the imagined space been maintained, the willingness of the participants to conjure up moments of the fantastical, and the differences between the imagined and the real became a site of self-reflection and analysis in their written accounts later (as quoted above). Just as a magician revealing the secrets involved in the creation of an illusion can heighten rather than belittle experience, this 'reveal' suggests how it significantly contributed to the discovery of meaning from the activity. From this we learn that it isn't necessary to actually encounter a dangerous situation, and perhaps a temporary illusion like watching a film or a performance can be sufficient enough for it to be an enduringly positive encounter with uncertainty. In this exercise, uncertainty generated an imaginative encounter that lingered even when the space was revealed as more mundane and evidence of previous occupants was obvious. The participants' reflections indicate that they were

Letting go of control

Uncertainty of the unknown was most extreme for Tom who participated in the exercise by not joining the human chain, and instead, waited for the group at the entrance to the undercroft. As one of the organizers of the workshop, he held greater responsibility for the participants' safety, and his explicit instructions for not going into the undercroft were ignored by the group, leaving him little choice but to wait for their return as he watched them disappear into the darkness. Upon reflecting on how he somatically experienced uncertainty, he considered how auditory cues from his uncontrollable pacing at the entrance of the undercroft might have communicated both the passage of time and a way for the participants to locate the direction of the exit. Two of the most provocative aspects of the activity were described as the 'sensory deprivation' (Hardwick in *Temple Works* 2015: 40) it offered and how 'time seemed to have disappeared' (Akama in *Temple Works* 2015: 9). In its place, the rhythmic quality of the sound of his walking could be seen as a proxy for his absence in the human chain. Tom wondered: 'As auditory information has the potential to dominate our perception of time, did my pacing significantly alter the perceived length of the activity? Also, given the lack of visual information, was a repetitive auditory cue used to maintain spatial orientation?' (Jackson in *Temple Works* 2015: 48). Tom's uncertainty was registered by the participants only afterwards, like Ann who acutely empathized with how he must have felt:

> Tom is alive with relief ahead of us, walking us out of the bunker area and only then really revealing how much it has cost him to let us go to a depth where [he] cannot see us, though we can see him. As the day goes on, the extent of the risk emerges: people have (allegedly) died lost; several hours of searching by the emergency services was necessary to extract earlier investigators. (Light in *Temple Works* 2015: 53)

Like the highly individualized accounts shared earlier, Tom's experience of uncertainty was unpleasant and discomforting, that came out of a collaborative activity while less physically connected to the group.

Tom later recovered and reflected (over a drink at a pub) how he was torn at the time when the group decided to descend into the undercroft, between extreme states of being risk-averse, worried for their safety, and also desiring the creativity and experimental experiences for a workshop that centred on uncertainty. These internal discords were born out of an unwanted sense of responsibility and a conflict of identity. He wished to freely participate in the activity, rather than moderate it and wanted to be perceived as a proponent of creative exploration, rather than as a voice of authority but felt bound by expectations regarding health and safety. We see here the tension and negotiation of ethics, and surrendering his control to ensure everyone's welfare was traded off between what the group consensually desired to explore. However, embracing rather than problematizing these tensions proved to be fruitful in Tom's later reflections on the day. With access to both his own memories and the written reflections produced by the other participants, these provided rich materials to further explore new ideas of uncertainty with regard to self-awareness, embodiment and identity.

The accounts above indicate various degrees of a willingness to surrender – to each other, to the condition, to the environment, to the encounter – even if that surrender also meant risk, discomfort, vulnerability and acute anxiety for some. There is also a surrendering of control and security by Tom as the host and organizer who felt he had to accede to the group's desire to go into a space that had precedent in being potentially dangerous. As the group shuffled further into the darkness, we observed surrendering of the visual, so predominant in our culture, to other senses, in the heightened smell and waft of the musty air, in the touch of each other's hands, in the feel of atmosphere, in the imaginations evoked and an overpowering embodiment of all the sensorial experiences. Knowledge of where they were, what time it was or what was factually surrounding the group seemed to matter little, confirmed by the disappointment some felt when the unknown environment was known when the lights were thrown on to it. Normative and orientating structures like time seemed to warp: 'bringing us to being in the present moment, so rare to be totally focused' (Akama in *Temple Works* 2015: 9). When social norms make any touching uncomfortable, especially between adults, genders and strangers, the very act of holding hands was a powerful demonstration of trust and intimacy and perhaps a surrendering of self to one another. It was such trust in one another and the touch of a person's hand that made the precarious and disorientating exploration possible.

The building exuded a smell of decay. The location and environment thus played a significant role, further facilitating the willingness of the workshop participants to surrender control. *Temple Works* is an 'industrial ruin', different from the usual places we inhabit. Edensor (2007: 217) describes that in such places, 'the body is generally liberated from the usual self-conscious performative constraints of the city' and instead, is permitted to engage in 'playful, experimental and unhindered interaction'. Not only did the sensory experience of the building communicate that this was a space free from the usual systems of control, it was also clearly introduced as such in the welcome talk by Susan Williamson, in telling us, that *Temple Works* is one of 'the origins of the spirit of outrageous invention' and intends to facilitate 'extreme performance rather than touristic art'. She proudly shared how the building is frequently used in vampire, zombie, sci-fi, gothic photo shoots and how they had hosted the largest punk and metal event in it. The appropriation of its surface as a canvas for a work of urban art and the haptic experience of navigating the remnants of past artistic performances all invited us to experience and engage with it as a place for creative expression.

Tracing

The notion of 'tracing' emerged after the participants undertook 'preparing' and 'sensing' stages of uncertainty, and the group reflected and discussed how 'capturing' uncertainty might be achieved, especially the undercroft activity they just experienced. Other than some photographs taken (see Helen Thornham's photo in *TempleWorks* 2015: 57), there was no documentation created in the undercroft. Over lunch the group decided to abandon 'capturing' as an idea, as it seemed to be contradictory to the very notion of uncertainty, and instead, 'tracing' was suggested as a more useful term to reflect the processual, dynamic and temporal aspects of uncertainty. This concept is coherent with the notion of the video trace (Pink 2011) that described the ways that video recording was used in the *Spaces for Innovation* and *Myths of the Near Futures* workshops discussed in Chapter 4. In the *Temple Works* workshop, the notion of tracing was significant since this insight enabled us to step away from the impossibility of capturing the unknown, towards marking uncertainty's emergent nature in a generative way. This constituted a transition from a closed to an open way of addressing uncertainty as we all brought our practices to bear in creating these traces – audio recordings, acoustic performances, photographs, rubbing texture of walls, poetry and video making. (Akama in *Temple Works* 2015: 7)

While such traces then became curated into *Temple Works* (2015), the section below selects and combines three traces explored in words, sounds and photographs, all of which became part of the process through which uncertainty was engaged as a technology. This means that these various materials, practices, objects and methods, can also become ways to accompany, orientate, attune and attend to uncertainty, and indeed it is when they combine with uncertainty that its generative potential as a technology begins to be activated. The acts of creating such traces, as it will become evident, are potent and evocative in inviting viewers to imagine what it might be like and enable a hermeneutical opening, suggested by Akama (2015: 270) as 'an in-between space of "this and that" world' so they can participate in a 'dynamic, active, changing, poetic immediacy'.

The creative practices of Simon Bowen (photography), Scott McLaughlin (acoustics) and Oz Hardwick (poetry) are significant to note because exploring and tracing uncertainty for them also invited a way to creatively respond to it through their own practices. We start with Simon's question 'How could I use photography to evoke our fumbling in the dark?' (Bowen in *Temple Works* 2015: 16), referring to the groups' undercroft adventure. In pursuing this question, Simon found a room with a few obstacles, including several chairs and pillars, and asked five willing volunteers to blindfold themselves using someone's scarf. He placed a smartphone in their back pockets and asked each person to walk from one end of the room to another with the obstacles in-between. While this setup does not seek to replicate the undercroft space or its experience, it enabled the group to re-engage with familiar elements of it again. The light carried in the volunteers' back pockets was made visible through long-exposure photography, tracing a line of light that wiggles across a semi-dark room: 'Certainly for the five volunteers and those watching, the resulting images evoked the characteristics of their individual blindfolded journeys, and (I hope) the stuttering, probing, misdirecting sensations of uncertainty more generally' (Bowen in *Temple Works* 2015: 16). The volunteers' reflections on uncertainty in relation to this experience are intriguing: 'The results of my participation in the activity made me reflect upon my own spatial awareness and I also wondered if those who found the task particularly challenging were left feeling uncertain about their reliance on visual perception?' (Jackson in *Temple Works* 2015: 48). The act of tracing uncertainty, turning something formless into form, opens up its re-translation (see colour Figure 5.3): 'Our clumsy groping and stumbling turns into a graceful movement of light through Simon's camera. They are indeed beautiful traces of uncertainty' (Akama in *Temple Works* 2015: 11).

Attempts to trace uncertainty involved manipulating and orchestrating various technical elements, whether they were 'multiple adjustments made in camera, exposure and development' (Bowen in *Temple Works* 2015: 16), or even writing things down in a notebook. Oz shares how traces of his writing were 'slightly awkward', not only physically 'in a hand-held notebook as I walked around the room', but also the act of listening and writing: 'Both listening and writing require degrees of attention that are not sustainable simultaneously, and negotiating unfamiliar space added a further demand upon my attention. Consequently, the partially-written phrases would often remain incomplete as my attention was caught by something else and I forgot what I was writing' (Hardwick in *Temple Works* 2015: 43). Yet, it is interesting to note that, in creating such traces, it is this lack of accuracy, perfection and the act of accommodating serendipity that also seems significant in remaining faithful to uncertainty. This is a form of surrender to the conditions. Oz continued to explain: 'I am fairly sure – though, of course, it is impossible to check – that within these shifts of attention I will have slipped in misapprehended homophones and, I expect, words that I just thought ought to have been there. This caused both frustration and intrigue in roughly equal measures' (ibid.). Incompleteness, misapprehension, forgetting and slipping here can be seen as a re-translation of an encounter that generates a different quality, but not framed as failures. Indeed, as emphasized by Pink (2011) in relation to video, just as the re-viewing of video cannot take us 'back' to the moments when it was recorded, or even to the same circumstances in which it might have been previously viewed, we likewise cannot reproduce the same feelings that have been experienced before. Like Simon Bowen's photographic traces of uncertainty, the acts of writing by Oz are similar attempts of turning something formless into form that changes the experience of uncertainty:

> My intention to listen to the 'voice' of the building soon became more specifically attuned to the way in which it transformed the voices of other workshop participants into an unintelligibly distorted murmur, above which sentences, phrases or single words would rise to clarity, sometimes discretely, at other times overlapping. The effect was of the architectural space translating a shared experience into a fragmentary, unstable monologue in, as it were, a single voice. (Hardwick in *Temple Works* 2015: 43)

Such fragments, literally, were written on square, coloured post-it notes and shared with the group (see colour Figure 5.4).

Another trace by Scott McLaughlin explores how 'sound can read space overtly, to step outside our sound's usually passive role in space, allowing sound to make space "unknown"' (McLaughlin in *Temple Works* 2015: 59). He invited the group to explore the acoustics of the engineering marvel of the two-acre space (see colour Figure 5.5) – rumoured to be once the largest room in England or even the world that housed the industrial looms bathed in natural light from the massive skylights – and experiment with ways to sense the volume and scale of this space through the spatial and temporal qualities of sound. The group wore the hard hats and spread themselves far around the main room, avoiding the joists that Susan warned were dangerous because the metal cables between each column have been known to snap. The group then formed a big 4-point star, keeping Scott in the middle with the shotgun mike. Ann recalls: 'We are in a safe uncertainty and we are interpreting and shaping, sounding and making. It is not a plan, but again two sets of discussions have converged on a course of action that involves us all' (Light in *Temple Works* 2015: 54). The group, having undertaken several uncertain experiences together during most of the day, was already conditioned to improvise and 'clap in an unpredictable sequence' (ibid.), united in exploring an uncertain experience, not by holding hands this time but by clapping asynchronously. Scott continues:

> One by one, each person made a single loud hand-clap, with the next person allowing the sound to decay fully before they made their own sound … the depth of the space is clearly audible from the long reverberation.

The broadband noise spectrum of each single clap fills the space like a shockwave. Dulled by the energy-sapping distance of the reflections, the sound roars and recedes in time like a tide-wave, as though squeezed by the far-off concrete surfaces. (McLaughlin in *Temple Works* 2015: 59)

The tracing of this activity and experience through audio 'reports a person and a space' (ibid.) as well as the walls, floor, ceiling and the volume of air contained within. 'Each is an action that energises the contained air and allows the room to describe itself. The people sound variously near and far, weaker and stronger claps, and each clap alternates with the voice of the space for several seconds after' (ibid.). The tracing is audial and temporal but it is also felt in people's bodies: 'A chain-reaction of reverb words travels through my body. The building joins in our chorus. Something releases in me – I am air and I am light – giddy with pleasure and wonderment of this shared moment. It's bloody awesome' (Akama in *Temple Works* 2015: 10).

Such traces through photographs, audio recordings and writing invite curiosity, perhaps because they are incomplete and retain a sense of an unknown. What is that wiggling light? What does that sentence mean? What does that space sound and feel like? These materials (see the curated outcomes in *Temple Works* 2015) imbue some enigma to draw a viewer in and look inquisitively at these traces – this enigma is similar to that of the undercroft that compelled the participants to explore it. This curiosity for the unknown echoes much of creative practice, including design research, to hold incomplete, nebulous and conflicting ideas together as part of progressing work (Lawson 2004). The material traces that were created remain faithful to the uncertainty that triggered their inception, maintaining the unknown and an openness. Some experiences were traced visually, some sonically and others through movement and writing. Consciously or otherwise, every trace was born out of a process that would always create unpredictable results: audio recordings in which both the building and the participants generated sounds without instruction; time-lapse videos which revealed patterns of movement unrecognizable at the time of their performance; and collages made out of building detritus which crumbled and disintegrated into new intriguing forms. The resulting collection of materials offers a fractured and incomplete record of the day. Yet surrendering resolution and absolutes can communicate different aspects of the experience and are appreciable in different ways, enticing further experimentation and open-ended meaning-making. Seen this way, they are productively ambiguous in drawing people in an interpretive relationship. Interaction design researchers, Gaver, Beaver and Benford (2003), describe the appeal of ambiguity as 'thwarting easy interpretation' because it requires people to actively participate in meaning-making. They continue:

> This can involve the integration of previously disconnected discourses, the projection of meaning onto an unspecified situation, or the resolution of an ethical dilemma. In each case, the artefact or situation sets the scene for meaning-making, but doesn't prescribe the result. Instead, the work of making an ambiguous situation comprehensible belongs to the person, and this can be both inherently pleasurable and lead to a deep conceptual appropriation of the artefact. (ibid.: 235)

Such productive ambiguity invites ownership rather than an impermeable, inviolable object that excludes and resists. The surrender of completeness means it is always open, porous and accessible.

Discovering capacity

The examples discussed in the earlier sections of this chapter focus on the process of making possibilities. This is not an explicit form of change-making in the sense of seeking to alter an already existing thing into a predetermined imagined other. Indeed the types of change-making that such opening up of possibilities entail do not involve making alternative routes or ranges of solutions to a problem. Rather they represent the discovery of capacities in each individual through a process of collective exploration. These possibilities were generated within each participant, catching some by surprise, overcoming fear and discomfort for some others, or reaffirming a few participants of their ability for trust and openness in precarious conditions. Here, we see how uncertainty was generative of forms of both individual and collective experiences that could not be predetermined, and that was specifically emergent from the configurations of things, processes and relationalities that formed the circumstances of the *Temple Works* workshop. This interrelatedness of various elements is articulated well by Simon Bowen:

> Of course I was not alone in my uncertainty – everybody met at least one new person and encountered one new practice. But this meeting was fruitful (as these reflections attest), which makes me reflect on how we dealt with our uncertainties of self, and what this might say about creative collaboration more generally. My traces experiment offers an analogy of how I approached my personal uncertainty: the 'blindfoldees' trusted me (and others present), acted (walked, probed), and were open to the consequent experiences. Similarly, I placed my trust in my fellows, made photographs (and a rationale for their making), and was open to how others might use them (and I, their work). (Bowen in *Temple Works* 2015: 16)

As seen here, generative forms of uncertainty assisted participants to hold themselves available to others – to be surprised, to be challenged, to be changed (Rose 2004). Similarly, Helen Thornham discovered how enjoyment can be part of uncertainty and there is a sense of catching herself in the moment of being amazed by it: 'I find that I am enjoying myself. There is also something about the griminess, the dirt, the pigeon smell from under arches in the rain, the provocation to do something – that I am really enjoying. It feels decadent and indulgent. This is also a sensory ghost I didn't know about until that moment' (Thornham in *Temple Works* 2015: 67). Likewise, this chancing upon locating enjoyment within uncertainty is also noticed by Akama:

> Who would've thought we could have this much fun. … Susan is a proud custodian of 'extreme performances' in this building, and we all now know why. Ann and I spot the Temple Works rooftop through the window of our train heading for London. I smile remembering the story about the lawn-mowing sheep. I feel like we've been changed by this encounter with the building and each other, but I can't quite put a finger on how. (Akama in *Temple Works* 2015: 11)

The changes that are noticed do not pertain just to the individual, but this changing means also to accompany the changing of the environment. 'Layers of meaning revealed as the paint peels and the rust bubbles. The building "perdures" (Ingold 2013) – always and already on its way to becoming something else' (Bowen in *Temple Works* 2015: 15). As Simon reflected, we too are always and already on our way to becoming something else. Oz Hardwick also observed:

The uncertainty here is apparent: what would I hear and how accurately could I transcribe it? What has particularly stayed with me so far about the experience, though, is an awareness of that temporal slip between thought and inscription. It's something that, through more than half a century of practice – particularly as my sense of myself is, to a significant degree, as a writer – has long since acquired the appearance of being akin to reflex; yet intense focus on process within the moment has paradoxically led to an acute awareness of the uncertainty of what that moment actually bears. 'Now' becomes a point of both infinite accumulation and infinite dispersal, and inscription becomes an uncertain act of remembrance of uncertainty, a tentative elegy for something impossible to have known. (Hardwick in *Temple Works* 2015: 43)

The ways that uncertainty emerged, was experienced, registered or traced, and reconstituted in this workshop were not predetermined, in that they were contingent on the precise circumstances of *Temple Works* and its affordances for the particular individuals and collective involved. We have seen how the workshop participants improvised with the materials, sensations, environment and relations within their grasp to create specific outcomes that intentionally transgressed regulatory guidance. We see how uncertainty was explored by improvising forms of safety that emerged from their capacity to surrender to the collective and collaborative sensibilities, modes of curiosity and exploration. Yet, we emphasize that the uncertainty that has been discussed in this chapter was not simply an unorchestrated or serendipitous encounter, but rather it was intentionally produced, if not precisely shaped by the facilitators of the workshop and pushed further by the participants. Framed as part of the *Design+Ethnography+Futures* series, the workshop had the making of forms of uncertainty at the core of its agenda and all were complicit in both its making and its using to generate new ways of knowing and sensing. To close this chapter, in the next section we reflect on what can be learnt and taken forward from this example.

Trusting

In the previous chapter we demonstrated how uncertainty can serve as a technology for disruption. In this chapter we have shown how when workshop participants collectively surrender to the uncertainties of disruption, particular forms of making can emerge. It is interesting to note how both disruption and surrender can suffer destructive connotations and outcomes. Acknowledging this, as we discussed previously, it is important to commit to co-explore change-making with people, rather than subjecting them alone to such conditions and feelings. The extreme forms of discomfort, confrontation, tension and precariousness observed in this workshop was embraced only because the group and facilitators consensually agreed to explore together, knowing full well that such consequences might become part of their collective encounter. Some may criticize that such uneasy experiences are best avoided, but when committing to an exploration of uncertainty, we in fact see these dimensions mirroring the diversity and richness of life. By embracing uncertainty, and especially being careful and attentive of how disruption and surrender can be structured, it means as researchers or practitioners engaged with future-making, we can build a sensitivity towards a plural, wider range of feelings, experiences and states of being rather than always ensuring pleasurable, convenient, efficient, useful or productive outcomes. At least in mainstream design, favourable qualities are always preferred to the point where unfavourable ones are designed out, partly to satisfy the agenda of the commissioning party and also to ensure design can 'sell' its value – what Dunne and Raby (2013) call 'affirmative design'. While this is not a new critique in design or elsewhere in technology discourses, the distinct difference in our *Design+Ethnography+Futures* workshops was not about critiquing at a distance and discussing these issues theoretically, but to viscerally feel what uncertainty can enable by directly experiencing, embracing and strategizing disruption and surrender. This echoes a similar commitment that Ann Light (2011: 436), a fellow explorer of several *Design+Ethnography+Futures* workshops, also makes in HCI 'to encompass the widest range of expression and experience' so that design and technology can 'remain more relevant and progressive in a world of different and shifting norms, and in a world where we would like norms to shift'. Thus, to embrace uncertainty is to avoid reproducing the status quo.

As such we argue that uncertainty, when coupled with disruption and surrender, enables the opening of new possibilities for participants – for action, experience and making. In taking up these possibilities, the participants in this workshop did not simply articulate alternative futures or contiguous presents, but rather delved into experiencing the present in ways that were more open and sought ways to trace this and to generate ways to sustain or 'keep' these experiences by bringing them to life again through the workshop and in a book publication. As we observed, embracing uncertainty and learning from the emergent relies upon trust – in the process and in one another – and a sense of optimism and confidence that *something* will come through. This approach seems fruitful in orienting towards future-making. These embodied elements of uncertainty and the ways in which we surrender to it are integral to processes of transformation and of remembering. Uncertainty was harnessed as an enabling technology, that during its course, also wove a route through the unique place that offered an alternative way to experience and learn from the collectivity of participants. As we discuss in the next chapter, developing ways in which to participate in, articulate and generate alternative ways of sensing and knowing also offers us a means by which to move beyond what is known towards imagining new and emergent futures.

6

Uncertainty as Technology for Moving Beyond

David Carlin, Yoko Akama, Sarah Pink and Shanti Sumartojo

Figure 6.1 A parody of certainty. Photo by Yoko Akama.

In this chapter we consider a third affordance of uncertainty – that of *moving beyond*. In doing so we build on the arguments developed in the previous two chapters – that uncertainty might be engaged as a technology for disruption and for surrender – and to understand moving beyond as a third element of this process. In doing so we focus on how uncertainty can afford ways of considering and approaching what is possible and emergent, and how it makes possible an anticipatory orientation that enables proposals for future actions.

Our notion of moving beyond is related to the approach to emergence we outlined in Chapter 1, following the anthropologist, Bill Maurer (2005: 4) who explains that 'you do not know where it is going ... but [you] go along for the ride, in mutual, open-ended and yet limited entanglements'. In going along for the ride, in surrendering control of the journey or destination, one moves beyond what is known into uncertain terrain with undetermined outcomes.

Participating in such a process requires purposeful engagement, and consequently this learning demands reflexivity and close attention to the detail of experience. Anthropology and design are both fields that acknowledge the importance of situated, embodied and lived accounts, rather than those of a detached observer, and as such both practices should recognize their positions as already entangled within and implicated in the sites they perform.

In this chapter we take a double step towards moving beyond. On the one hand we take as our focus the example of *Essaying the FabPod* workshop, which specifically developed a process through which we sought to go beyond the ways that we had previously experienced, thought and imagined an architecturally designed acoustic meeting space. On the other, in discussing this we go beyond the conventions of academic writing.

Conventions in academic papers often privilege empirical 'matters of fact' rather than realism on 'matters of concern' (Latour 2008). This makes it particularly difficult to 'capture' emergence, change and transformation, especially those that cannot be documented 'objectively' on a video or interview transcripts (Akama 2015) or to express emergent processes such as those discussed in relation to the video trace (Pink 2011) discussed in Chapter 1 and the 'trace' discussed in Chapter 5. In writing, Akama (2015) suggests we might re-inscribe this sense of emergence into our reporting through ficto-critical writing and brief-but-vivid narratives to accentuate moments and perceptions that are highly personal. In this chapter, a creative non-fiction writer, David Carlin, and design researcher, Yoko Akama, take the lead in straying from academic norms of writing adhered to commonly in disciplines including design and anthropology, in an attempt to open up ways of thinking about the not-yet-known and make possible new propositions. This too is a form of moving beyond, embracing modes of writing and composition in which uncertainty is openly staged, and in which it is activated as a technology, as discussed in Chapter 3.

Non-fiction creative writing

In co-writing this and the next four sections ('Why the *FabPod*?', 'An essaying methodology', 'Methods' and 'Moving beyond'), David and Yoko draw on a workshop called *Essaying the FabPod*. This workshop was led by David, a creative writer working in the literary non-fiction forms of essay and memoir. It was through experimenting in modes of creative non-fiction writing that workshop participants explored their relationship to a prototypical meeting enclosure called the *FabPod*. As with other *Design+Ethnography+Futures* workshops, David was invited through collegial friendship and because of his ongoing critical engagement with non-fiction as, in the terms of the argument of this book, a technology of uncertainty. We intend not only to articulate the emergent relations generated by the use of uncertainty as an organizing principle in investigating the *FabPod*, but also to stage a strategic 'moving beyond' the conventions of academic writing mentioned above. For instance, perhaps, by speaking of ourselves in the first person, something scarcely radical in the academy these days but more complicated to do when writing collaboratively – are we singular, plural or in-between, in dialogue or in unison? These explorations deliberately feature in this chapter through the voice, tone and style of writing.

Chapter 2 of this book discusses some of the intersections between the concepts of risk and uncertainty. Now, bringing non-fiction creative practice into the disciplinary mix alongside design and anthropology, a different connection with risk comes into view: the potential for *essaying* (see Lane Kauffmann 1988) to help create what Latour calls 'risky accounts'. For Latour, 'a risky account, mean[s] that it can easily fail – it does fail most of the time – since it can put aside neither the complete artificiality of the enterprise nor its claim to accuracy and truthfulness' (Latour 2005: 133). In the *Essaying the FabPod* workshop a group of twelve invited creative writers, designers, ethnographers, and non-fiction media makers made a collection of risky accounts in relation to the *FabPod* (Carlin et al. 2015). Or, perhaps more accurately, the collection itself became a collaboratively produced risky account, one which mobilized uncertainty as a technology to uncover knowledge about the *FabPod* that goes beyond what might be produced by more conventional approaches. The collection produced from the day's activities was subtitled: 'An improvised experimental collaborative account of the uncertain cultural life and futures of the *FabPod* as of August 21 2014' (*Essaying* 2014). The playfulness of this subtitle both gestures with an ironic nod towards anachronistic conventions of scientific discourse and insists on a precisely delimited scope: this, it claims, is only what was uncovered in relation to the *FabPod*, by this group of researchers, using these methods, on this day. The account is risky, in Latour's terms, because it embraces completely artificial (or, as we might say in creative arts and design: *makerly*) methods of irony, speculation, metaphor and fabulation, among others, while at the same time asserting that these methods can produce something true and accurate about the object under investigation. As such, this method also speaks to the other two major themes of the book, disruption and surrender, in that it subverted academic convention and was a means by which those participants who were novice non-fiction writers could surrender to a new practice of inquiry (see Chapter 3).

In order to describe the *FabPod* workshop, David and Yoko combine description of how David prepared for the workshop, and reflect on how we both experienced it, with creative writing pieces that hint at and re-inscript how moving beyond was viscerally felt. In doing so, it comments on uncertainty as technology for moving beyond in three ways: first, it introduces the methods developed by David and performed by the participants as a technology for extending and exceeding how we already understood the *FabPod* and its possibilities, in which we acknowledge and account for how human and non-human participation was critical, including the imaginary and actual role of the *FabPod*. Secondly, the creative writing in this chapter is another method 'improvised' by David and Yoko to create a hermeneutical opening, an 'in-between space' of 'this and that' world to participate in a 'dynamic, active, changing, poetic immediacy' (Akama 2015, quoting Pilgrim 1986: 270). The intention is to evoke the emergent unfolding of the workshop experience from different, immersed perspectives. This approach echoes the creative writing produced as an e-book by the twelve participants during *Essaying the FabPod* workshop (see Miles and Carlin 2014). Thirdly, the chapter articulates the kind of moving beyond that enabled participants in the workshop to create, share and speak (write) from collectively produced positions and ways of knowing.

Why the *FabPod*?

The *FabPod* is an ambitious experiment of various hyperbolic curvatures, with modular construction and materials for noise diffusion. A prototype for a meeting space, it stands in RMIT's Design Hub building for use and further iteration by its interdisciplinary team of creators, researchers from the fields of acoustic design, architecture, digital fabrication and craft (http://www.sial.rmit.edu.au/portfolio/fabpod-sial/). The original *FabPod* project grew out of observations of the acoustic properties of the hyperbolic surfaces in the interior of Gaudi's Sagrada Familia Church in Barcelona, where RMIT researchers from the Spatial Information Architecture Laboratory (SIAL) had, at that time, a leading role.

The *FabPod* is constructed from curved pieces of fabric, metal and transparent windows that fit together into an intriguing form that affords some visual privacy for people inside it; it is pierced by small porthole windows so that those inside are visible, but this requires people outside to purposefully peer in (see colour Figure 6.2). It stands in a warehouse-style open-plan office of hard surfaces of concrete, steel and glass that make acoustics difficult to manage, inhibiting the collaborative practices the warehouse space aimed to foster. The *FabPod* was intended as a comfortable eight-member meeting room that diminished the sound of people speaking, providing some acoustic privacy by scattering and absorbing sound, and its makers describe it as a 'prototype meeting enclosure located in an open knowledge space ... developed to address acoustic performance ... bringing together existing knowledge of acoustic diffusion, cnc prototyping and digital workflows and craft traditions of making' (Williams et al. 2013: n.p.).

The *FabPod* is thus a 'futuristic', propositional architectural object, designed using complex mathematical equations and constructed from innovative, modular materials. Placed in the middle of the open floor of the RMIT Design Hub Level 9 workspace, it is singular in appearance, to say the least, and, to the lay observer, unexplained. As researchers and research support staff in various multi-disciplinary teams unrelated to the *FabPod* project began to occupy the surrounding open-plan spaces on Level 9 when the Design Hub first became operational, they encountered the *FabPod* as a 'found object'. They might know more, less or nothing at all about the *FabPod*'s status as an outcome of exceptional interdisciplinary research into acoustic diffusion, digital fabrication, material customization technology and architectural geometry (see colour Figures 3.3 and 6.2).

David was one such cohabitant of Level 9 with the *FabPod* for a time, working on a research project housed in close proximity to it. Like others he was intrigued by the bold incongruity of its presence, all bulging curves, glowing circular 'eyes' and quilt of colours (purples, greens and greys), within the otherwise angular, *ubermensch* austerity of the building's interior environment. However, David's experience of the *FabPod* as a meeting space echoed those of many other users who were disappointed by its acoustic performance and the promises it seemed to make of providing privacy for conversations inside the structure. Despite its unique and striking features in shape, material, structure and aesthetics – aspects that that made it a must-see show-piece for guests who visited RMIT University – its everyday use was often fraught. In the interior space of the *FabPod*, the effect of being enclosed by its unique, hyperboloid, undulating walls was contradicted by the dominance of two large black, distinctly rectangular tables, which had been used by the architectural team to lay out plans when constructing the *FabPod* and then later discovered were too large to be removed through the curved entranceway. There was also a large, visually dominant (and again, of course, rectangular) screen designed for videoconferencing that was notoriously difficult to use.

Despite its purported function of providing acoustic privacy for meetings in an open-plan workspace, Yoko and Sarah's curiosity for considering the *FabPod* as a potential site, experience or 'object' for a *Design+Ethnography+Futures* workshop was triggered by overheard accounts. Users of the prototype were often disgruntled with the *FabPod* as a meeting room in terms of its noise-diffusing acoustics. The experience of using it was also marred by low light levels, and many were disappointed by the design and technological 'promises' it appeared to make by its presence, promises it did not fulfil in its perceived acoustic properties. Prior to the workshop, Yoko, Sarah and their research assistant Annie began to explore how it was perceived and experienced through a video ethnography of its users, which sought to examine their past, recent and imagined future experiences of the meeting space. In an interview about the *FabPod*, for example, one user described 'how he was initially fascinated by it, but "not being able to stay in it" due to its darkness that made it impractical as a meeting room. Others also seemed unconvinced by how it affected sounds made by people inside it: "you start questioning the privacy of the space'" (Akama et al. 2015: 535). Given its status as a prototype, often such feedback would be used to inform the next iteration of the design, to iron out its acoustic issues and improve upon them. However, the *Design+Ethnography+Futures* approach departed from this 'convention' to embark on ways to disrupt the definition of the *FabPod* as a meeting space and the ways in which this proscribed the user experiences of it. This presented an opportunity to explore uncertainty through the *FabPod*, including in our own pre-conceptions of what it is and what it could become.

The experience of being-with and using the *FabPod* has variously contradicted, extended or seemed to have surpassed what its designers had envisaged. This is not uncommon for design and architectural projects and their subsequent occupation and elaboration by human and non-human actors. These have emerged in Human–Computer Interaction and Participatory Design discourses as 'design for unanticipated use' or 'design-after-design' (see Moran 2002; Björgvinsson et al. 2012) to accommodate and prompt ways for new imaginings through use. However, the quirky and heightened dissonance of the *FabPod* as a structure, bringing echoes of the mathematical genius of Gaudi to a distant university site of research innovation, set up fertile conditions for a workshop that sought to play with and unsettle the status and meaning of the *FabPod* by generating new types of essayed experiences within, around and beyond it, a process fundamentally animated by uncertainty. The *Essaying the FabPod* workshop, as David and Yoko discuss in this chapter, allowed us to explore what other possibilities could be imagined and sensed by humans in relation to the *FabPod*. Through a fluid and playful process of negotiation, self-reflexive observation, speculation, listening, writing and embodied interaction, the workshop explored how creative writing, and in particular an *essaying* methodology, could provoke people to re-imagine, discuss and interrogate an architectural artefact. In design terms, the aim was not to imagine and propose alterations to the *FabPod* structure or user experience, but rather to open up a broader palette of perspectives as to what the *FabPod* was *doing*; what it was suggesting or producing through effects of uncertainty.

An essaying methodology

The workshop took place on 21 August 2014 over three hours, attended by twelve participants. The majority of the participants were researchers from the non/fictionLab at RMIT University, an interdisciplinary creative arts research group. Alongside these writers, poets, film theorists and media makers were anthropologists, sociologists and designers. The workshop was intended to be 'deliberately intensive, brief, provisional and risky. The intent was to contribute to an ongoing project investigating the future of the *FabPod*, and to test an agile, multidisciplinary research method that hovered precariously between the creative, critical and clumsy' (Miles in *Essaying* 2014: 3). The notion of uncertainty underpinned the workshop in various ways. For some the *FabPod* itself was an uncertain object; for others who were not writers (of poetry, fiction or creative non-fiction), creative writing put them on uncertain ground.

The concept of the 'essaying' workshop methodology as developed here by David (and elaborated in other contexts with writer Francesca Rendle-Short and film essayist John Hughes) draws from theories and practices of the essay in the long tradition of Montaigne's (1993) 'Que sais-je?' ('What do I know?'). Although the essay has come to mean, in many contexts, such as schools and universities, an authoritative account that attempts to make a coherent and rigidly structured argument about a given subject, the tradition of what has been called the 'personal essay' (Lopate 1995) runs contrary to this. As can be seen from Montaigne's question, the (personal) essay begins not from certainty but from doubt: in fact, as David Shields has put it, 'the essay enacts doubt' (Shields 2010: 139). The essayist uses their embodied self as a filter to examine 'how the world comes at [them]' (Lopate 1995: xxvii). Because the filter is a human being, it is partial, prone to blockages and misdirections, prey to the dispositions of its history, memory, and bodily and sensory configurations. The technique of 'essaying' is the endeavour – by necessity, speculative, tentative and inconclusive – to make an account of such a contingent encounter with an object, which might in itself be an event, a text, an atmosphere, a memory or some combination of such objects. Or in this instance, a 'FabPod'. The essay form has in the past forty years found renewed vitality in literary and audiovisual forms including the lyric essay (see Tall and D'Agata 1997) and the video essay (Bresland 2014), and is sometimes given the generic name 'creative non-fiction' (although this is contested; see Carlin and Rendle-Short 2013). 'Creative non-fiction', writes Mary Cappello insightfully, 'appreciates the power of prepositions. Instead of writing *about*, as in "what is your book about?", it writes *from*. Or nearby, towards, under, through, and so on. Rather than mean, it does. It animates. A process and a set of relations more than anyThing' (Cappello 2013: 66). This invitation to write or otherwise respond creatively from a position of 'thinking prepositionally' (Rendle-Short 2012: 6) is pivotal to the essaying methodology, as shall be seen in discussion here of the *FabPod* essaying workshop, where we wrote, talked and moved first in isolation from, and then beside and inside the *FabPod*, aiming to make and record a set of relations with it. Above all we began with the principle that we were uncertain but curious about what would happen that day.

Methods

The workshop was divided into two symmetrical halves, 'outside' and 'inside/beside'. Some of the workshop participants were very familiar with the *FabPod*, having worked alongside it (as discussed above) and/or having known more or less about the theoretical propositions underlying its design and construction. One of the *FabPod*'s designers was able to join in on the early section of the workshop. Other participants knew little if anything about the *FabPod*, its purpose, history or physical form. The workshop aimed to explore the generative capacity of this *spectrum of uncertainty*. Accordingly, the first half of the workshop was held in a space adjacent to, but physically removed from, the *FabPod*, and participants were not able to see or access the *FabPod* at this time. The moment of direct encounter was delayed and instead the *FabPod* was indirectly encountered through its affective and cognitive traces collected in and by the workshop participants.

Method 1: Participants are instructed to arrange themselves into a line, with at one end, the person who knows most about the *FabPod*, and at the other, the person who knows least (Figure 6.1). Participants need to negotiate on their feet whether each knows more or less than someone else; as with a citizen jury, there is no external guide or pre-existing rules as to how to proceed. However, there is time pressure and advice from the facilitator to treat the task playfully, since by definition it is impossible to be certain about the 'correct' order or hierarchy of relative knowledge. On one level the task is absurd: this is part of the point of the exercise, to parody a regime of certainty.

Here's Yoko's take on this experience:

> *Bridget, Kyla, Francesca and Alvin haven't even seen the FabPod – how wonderfully delicious. Their anticipation for what it's like is very exciting – a bit like sharing the excitement before they unwrap a gift. Though, both Francesca and Alvin sheepishly admit that they've Googled it. Like selecting the gift on an on-line catalogue. It's impossible not to know anything these days. Sometimes, what doesn't exist or exists only in one's imagination can be felt as more real than real. Francesca says she doesn't want to see the FabPod because she's already anticipating her disappointment. I found out that Santa doesn't exist when I saw the roller-skates in the boot of my parents' car, but I pretended to be happy when it was given to me as a gift from Santa. We all have versions of such stories.*
>
> *We form pairs, triads or a quartet, a cross between speed-dating and a dance to find who our closest neighbours might be. I'm probably in the cluster of people who know a lot about the FabPod, but what do we know? I latch on to the feeling words I hear because they are another kind of knowing.*
>
> *Homely.*
> *Disappointment.*
> *Sorrow.*
> *Amusing.*
> *Pompous.*
> *Oddity.*
> *Curious.*
> *Affection.*
> *Serious.*
> *Whimsical.*
> *Aloof.*
> *Ambitious.*
> *Bits and pieces.*
> *Dark.*
> *Sleepy.*
>
> *It's a necklace of perceptions and sensations that defies categorization. A bit like the* FabPod. *Not about hyperbolic-whats-its. Those mathematical curvatures*

Uncertainty as Technology for Moving Beyond   113

of Gaudi's for acoustic diffusion. Some of these affective qualities are felt deeply and strongly.

And did we know what we know about the FabPod until that moment of articulation and comparison? How do I know more or less about its aloofness, compared to another person's affection? How certain am I about this knowing?

The lineup forms by following lay conventions – those who use the FabPod most frequently jostle for the 'top' position of knowing the most – a competition between Sarah, Adrian and myself. I'm pleasantly surprised and intrigued by what they both know. Adrian prattles on about something technical on noise and sound in a typical, Adrian-ish-spectrum-y way. He's so good with facts and logic, unlike me, and I find his reasoning totally fascinating. Sarah shares how it arrived in pieces and was assembled in situ, reminding her of the Tardis in Doctor Who. Witnessing this coincided with a new job at RMIT to sear it vividly in her memory. I don't remember FabPod's arrival other than the e-mail we got about the inconvenience it might cause by its construction on level 9, but I remember Sarah's arrival at RMIT and feeling a bit intimidated. She's not really. It's funny how these encounters are shaped and how something like the FabPod marks our place in the past and becomes part of our story.

We three are talking about knowing on different planes but settle comfortably in a row.

I take a photo finish (Figure 6.1).

Method 2: 'Knowledge Circle'. Participants organize themselves into a circle in the same order as the line they have just made together. Then each person, starting with the person who knows least and continuing in that order, tells what they know about the *FabPod*. It is very important that this order and vector be followed, precisely because it runs against normative practices of knowledge-sharing, wherein the 'expert' or person with most knowledge would simply brief the rest of the team. This method brings to the surface evidence of the heterogeneous responses to the object under discussion, which might otherwise tend to be erased or subsumed under the 'official' narrative of the expert (for instance, in this case, the designer of the *FabPod* who, as the person who knew most, was forced to speak last). This is not to make a fetish out of ignorance, but rather to enable the uncertain offcuts of knowledge, the affective surpluses or remainders, to be articulated to others and made available for further use, together with material evidence of various kinds. The method is also additive and inclusive: each person, even the least knowledgeable, is able to contribute something, however tentative and uncertain. Those more knowledgeable cannot repeat what has already been established or postulated, but only add new contributions to the highly contingent and fluid pool of knowledge. This approach resonates with the discussion in Chapter 2 in which expertise is a form of mitigating risk and demonstrating mastery. However, it can also be a form of counterweight to uncertainty that diminishes possibility and emergence, and thus limits future propositions.

Participants listen as each person speaks, and are invited to take notes if they like. David took the following notes on what he heard that struck him:

FabPod:

Some kind of device
We might be making it
Pod – cosy, home-y sense of belonging
I wanted it to be nothing
I want there to be sorrow
exhibit
room
one of the first things I saw at RMIT
spaceship
I didn't see the point of it
very colourful
roundedness
I like the way light gets in
funny: serious but also whimsical
physically familiar in my body
a landscape of the familiar
acoustically neutral
foible|pompous
Function: soundproof, but doesn't work
technology that doesn't work
argument maker
The FabPod *that is in cvs and on websites*
the people who made it > humourous, aloof, closed but want to be open
sits in a harsh masculine building
against Sean Godsell [Design Hub architect]> little battler
the plans are quite different from the reality
jigsaw

dull: makes you feel tired
gradually I've stopped going in there
voice feels flattened or exposed
Sagrada Familia> nave scaffolded for the Pope's visit > long reverberation time
but amazingly coherent sound
Gaudi's doubly curved surfaces
hyperboloid: cooling tower shape
space within a space
Swiss precision construction> digital fabrication techniques
when you intersect hyperboloids...
180 cells
made with student labour
designed lots of versions> chose the best
materials donated> recycled felt, aluminium

Method 3: Participants are invited to briefly make a 'data assemblage', making a heterogeneous list of all the keywords, ideas and thoughts that have struck them in listening to the collective narrative, above. From this data assemblage, they are invited to discern a central theme, governing idea or question that will form a focal point for their subsequent essaying practice.

Method 4: Participants write, for 25 minutes, and still from the space apart from direct contact with the *FabPod*, a short essay on the subject of the *FabPod* that takes account of the emergent focal point and the evidence generated by the preceding exercises of collaborative knowledge and uncertainty (see colour Figure 6.3).

[This completes the first half of the workshop.]

Method 5: Everyone (finally!) goes inside the warehouse where the *FabPod* sits, and enjoys a delicious smorgasbord lunch in and around the *FabPod*, in an informal 'being-alongside' the architectural artefact. Various discussions, and improvised experiments to test the acoustic properties of the *FabPod*, ensue.

Method 6: Participants write a second flash-essay, for another 25 minutes, this time from an embodied position either inside or beside the *FabPod*. In line with the concept of essaying as speculative non-fiction, participants are invited if they so choose to speculate as to future states of belonging for the *FabPod*.

Method 7: Although time is limited, at the end of the workshop the writings and the experience of making them are discussed and shared.

It would be a mistake to confuse the method's simplicity with the complexity of context it is performed within, a tendency of professional aspects of design and ethnography that often focus on systematic and technical elements of methods and their reporting. As suggested by Light and Akama (2012) in participatory design, there is no method until it is enacted because methods need embodiment. Following their argument, we need a more synthesized and dynamic reading to acknowledge how methods infuse with many other actors and elements. This may include the facilitator's – in this case David's – improvisations as an educator-researcher-writer-theatre-performer-artist that combined 'embodied savviness' and a 'delicate conviction in their bones' (Gibson in Carlin and Rendle-Short 2016: 451). Shanti, a participant of *Essaying the FabPod* workshop later reflected that the experience allowed her to notice how people and the *FabPod* are already assembled that 'include things around it (desks, computers, chairs), the materials that are made of (plastic, glass, metal, fabric), the changing internal meteorological conditions (light, sound, temperature) … engendered feelings, affects, maybe atmospheres' (Sumartojo in Carlin et al. 2015: 5). This connected to worlds imagined, virtual and futures. We may not be able to understand the exact configuration of these multiple, complex components, but it allowed us a moment to acknowledge our situatedness and interrelatedness and become part of this assemblage.

The potency of the workshop method was its simple but nuanced structure and openness as a container for multiple possibilities, the way its uncertainty generated new ways of thinking about the *FabPod* and its possibilities. The highly constrained protocols of the workshop, restricting time and movement, released participants to embrace uncertainty as an appropriate technology and to surrender to the workshop process. And by allowing participants to embrace its uncertain outcome, it allowed for unfiltered and associative elements to spontaneously emerge as knowing, often taking the person by surprise about what they thought they knew. This emergence of knowing the *FabPod* and our relation to it, means that our knowing might only matter in that moment and by those who participated processually in its sharing. This knowing was not the kind of publicly verifiable knowledge that is independent and can be detached from the person and context, but rather takes an intimate form.

This difference in knowing follows the heuristics proposed by a seminal American philosopher Thomas Kasulis (2002) that describes contrasting world-views as integrity and intimacy-oriented, where he proposes that one tends to dominate in certain cultures that then determines how we think about the world, ourselves and our society. Put simply, in an integrity-based model of knowing, the knower and known exist separately to assume a publicly verifiable objectivity. The emotions of the knower do not figure in the integrity-view, and in fact the knower can be interchangeable with any other knower. This allows knowledge to be replicable and transportable. In contrast, Kasulis suggests that the intimacy-view sees the knower and known overlap partly and internally, so that knowing about something means learning a little bit about the knower as well as the known; 'Knowledge is assimilated, not acquired' because it is 'absorbed into the body somatically through praxis' (Kasulis 2002: 79). Sharing of such knowledge means that knowers need be peers or belong to the same community to share similar praxis. This contrasts with the emphasis often given to understand epistemology by reading and writing following an academic practice to engage with theory, inculcating a bias for knowledge as one thing and not the other. The implication of a research method that adopts an intimacy-view is that it allows researchers to experience and embody different ways of knowing, with value for creative practice.

Indeed, the intimacy-view's knowing through doing is subject to emergent affects akin to those that imbue the ongoing and anticipatory mode of video-making or video as more-than-documentation, as we discussed in Chapter 1. This is important for our arguments about uncertainty as a technology because it recognizes the immaterial and felt (in both a bodily and affective sense) as an important part of how uncertainty might open up new possible futures. In the context of the workshops that this book discusses, it also extends ways of knowing to encompass and even rely on the involvement of other humans and non-humans – in other words, to cast forward by means of a way of knowing that is inherently collective, even when the results of such collaborative efforts are unknown.

Moving beyond

Documentations of the workshop as photography and video, and the results of our collaborative writing process – the collective *essaying* – were assembled and turned into an e-book designed and edited by Adrian Miles and David

Carlin and published in the journal *Axon* (Carlin et al. 2015). Adrian describes the collected essays and accompanying visual documentation as a 'transitory, quick and dirty research sketch', from which the outcomes are 'deliberately intensive, brief, provisional and risky' (Miles, 'Blurb' in Carlin et al. 2015: 3). The participants agreed and embarked upon this workshop with the understanding that this collective 'report' would be produced and published. The curation of materials into the e-book constitutes a bricolage that purposefully resists being read as a unified narrative or argument. Instead, the mini essays, placed into two sections, 'Outside' and 'Inside', vibrate between sketches of speculation, wonder, analysis, playful fancy, allegory and science fiction.

In the opening essay, Shanti Sumartojo finds herself asking questions such as 'If we think of [an object] as having a personality, what does that do to our stance towards it?' (*Essaying* 2014: 5). Shanti extends her discussion of the *FabPod* as a 'story of assemblage and connection' to consider the object's 'spatial and temporal embeddedness, purposefulness and affective charge', and this leads to playful speculation about the *FabPod* as an active, affective agent: 'Is it content? Does it sit easily with the people and objects around it? Is it mostly OK, but wishes it could change a few things, like that plant that tickles it or that jutting corner that makes a funny noise?' (ibid.: 6). The writing risks expressing a sense of tender empathy in animating what sociology might conventionally bracket off as an inanimate object. This enlivening or animation of the *FabPod* is a direction explored by a number of the following essays, such as here where it situates a reflection on the precarity of design intentions: 'It wants to be functional and helpful, this little creature, but it floats airily and almost useless in the density of a steel and concrete palace of design' (Carlin et al. 2015: 9).

A creative writer, Francesca Rendle-Short, pushes the form of the essay into '7 tries' (since 'essai', in French, means to attempt or try). Never having seen the *FabPod*, she has Googled it and fears she will be disappointed. The *FabPod*, for her, is an effect of language: 'It has to start with *it*, a referential pronoun. What is the it? What does it refer to? What are we all talking about?' Responding to the affective charge of the Design Hub atmosphere, and the stories of the *FabPod* leads Francesca to postulate, abruptly: 'I think the it in this case is about death. Hopes dashed. And yes, and sorrow too that does, that must come alongside, lurk there, here, sitting in the spots around it, speaking in strange acoustic, or should we say non-acoustic tones' (Rendle-Short 2015: 15). Here we can observe how the techniques of essaying elaborated in the workshop are working to engender what Kathleen Stewart calls 'atmospheric attunements' (2010: 4). Stewart writes:

> Attending to atmospheres and attunements to them is for me a lateral move. A sideways step into what normally gets stepped over, a curious pause to wonder what analytic objects might matter in the singularity of a situation and what forms of writing and thinking might approach them. An atmospheric attunement is an alerted sense that something is happening and an attachment to sensing out whatever it is. It takes place within a world of some sort and it is itself a generative, compositional worlding. (2010: 4)

This is a particular type of 'sideways step', a particular mode of 'curious pause', a technique to mobilize uncertainty to 'register the tactility and significance of something coming into form through an assemblage of affects, routes, conditions, sensibilities, and habits' (Stewart 2012: 524). Attending to uncertain processes, how they work and feel and what outcomes derive from them is precisely the double layering of uncertainty identified in Chapter 3 – that uncertainty as a technology might articulate quite differently in the imagination of different disciplines or practices; and how in turn uncertainty might impact on specific processes or activities. Furthermore, the attunement that Stewart describes recognizes the intimacy (Kasulis 2002) or mindfulness (Akama 2018) that connects uncertainty to surrender (see Chapter 5).

Another workshop participant, a widely published poet from Singapore, Alvin Pang, creates an ironic allegory between the *FabPod* and Singapore as a postcolonial nation state: 'Those privy to her history appreciate that she is easy to misread' (Pang in *Essaying* 2014: 19). Meanwhile, Adrian Miles, a media theorist, reflects on the cultural history of noise, and later experiments with 'the indifference of listing' inspired by Ian Bogost's (2012) notion of the ontograph. After lunch the mood changes and Yoko Akama fantasizes in her second essay about dozing off in the 'sanctuary' of the *FabPod*, before declaiming, in liberated disciplinary frustration:

> I wish the whole situation could be different. I wish the fabpod wasn't so precious and enabled anyone to interact with it, change it, customise it, augment it, live in it. I wish we could grow plants inside. I wish we could

have a silent disco. I wish we could take some of the panels out and replace it with something else. I wish the tables and screens could go. I wish we felt comfortable, even encouraged to do these things instead of being promised something else that doesn't actually deliver. I wish the fabpod let us be us – instead of being the embodiment of the creator. Its perception is its perfection. Precious. Serious research. God, I hate that about design. (Akama in *Essaying* 2014: 40)

And for some participants, such as David Carlin, the collaborative and situated processes of the day's workshop has shifted their perceptions: 'I used to think of the fabpod as a futuristic folly of a certain sort, wonderful but somehow with an air of hubris. Is it too much a product of cool intellect? But now I want to go there late at night, to make it coloured and to bounce music off its many navels' (Carlin et al. 2015: 52).

And what of the experiences of the instigators and facilitators, like David and Yoko? How is this methodology and outcome moved beyond, carried into other contexts and dimensions of their practices? Here are Yoko's thoughts:

Am-is-was-were: I don't even know what tense I'm supposed to write this in (David help!!) Many designers would admit that writing is not their strongest skill – drawing is-are-were their better asset. My grammar is terrible and I can't keep using the excuse that Japanese is my first language. I've been living outside of Japan from the age of 12. Now I live and work in Australia with a sprinkle of The Strain (urgh ...).

So here-there I was, immersing in an uncertain writing process, riddled with self-induced anxieties. I felt like an amateur cooking among Michelin chefs in a kitchen ... until it suddenly dawned on me, hearing everyone's spoken words that was so deliciously wonderful, that I had to let go and just go with the flow. Maybe it didn't matter if my grammar is-was imperfect, and maybe I can just doodle away, like I do when I draw or design. Maybe its perfection, completion and comprehensibility doesn't matter, just like drawing that allows ideas to form without-thinking. Seeing words and structure this way helped to tap into a 'muscle memory' of a different kind – a memory of generating ideas, imagining compositions, materializing a thought, but through words rather than images. Letting go and embracing uncertainty can generate many possibilities, like re-wiring a muscle memory for another kind of 'making'.

This alchemical change that started that day continues even now as I re-live that experience. As a designer who runs workshops all the time, I am drawn to methods and structures – to look at the nuts and bolts that make something work as well as the invisible stuff in-between. Out of all Design+Ethnography+Futures workshop, Essaying the FabPod was one of my favorites (coming close after Temple Works). I admire its beautiful simplicity in method and its pace that balanced intensity and freedom. I trusted the process that allowed the outcomes to be genuinely 'ours', whilst retaining our own flavours, like a good stew that harmonises the integrity of each ingredient. I take these learnings into my design practice – not the exact method, but the conceptual frameworks that inform them– to enrich what I can-will-might do in another place and time with other people.

And of course, I can never look, feel and experience the FabPod the same way again – now it is with much more affection.

And here are David's reflections:

It's funny that Yoko finds writing daunting. I mean, I find it daunting too but not nearly so daunting as drawing or singing or any number of other things. I've written elsewhere, with Francesca Rendle-Short (Carlin and Rendle-Short 2016) about a collaborative residency project we have worked on where the concepts of the gift and the invitation have been important. This struck me just now because it occurred to me that what Essaying the Fabpod *workshop offered me was the* gift *of the concept of uncertainty. Uncertainty is a technology that drives the type of nonfiction writing I do, as the writing attempts to push against the grain that aligns nonfiction with certainties (settled, unproblematic facts), in opposition to fiction, in which, supposedly, anything can happen. (Both poles of this binary set are of course more complicated and mutually implicated.) I had thought about this previously but without, as it were, putting uncertainty up in lights, as the headline act. Also, to think of it as a* technology *is new to me, like a new dance step. So my moving beyond is very different to yours, Yoko. I have been working for some time with essaying as, I suppose, a technology, to produce 'risky accounts', as we talked about above. But having* uncertainty *as the framing device for this workshop brought about a little epiphany, in collision with Montaigne the essayist's mantra, 'what do I know?' This was the idea of what I'm calling (as if it was a kind of sideshow act!) the 'spectrum of uncertainty'. I'd never tried this before. I've since used this particular technique of the spectrum of uncertainty in two very different workshop contexts – one with a group of artists, academics and tourism small-business people in Finland, the other with writers and students in Manila.*

Both times it worked beautifully to unearth a patchwork of unrehearsed stories, observations and images pertaining to the shared object of inquiry – in

Finland this was the nascent concept of a 'slowlab', while in Manila it was the city itself. This opened up a space that – what? Here, my notebook is suddenly cluttered with crossings out, false starts and stuttering attempts at coherent summary ... the effort towards a unified, solo-voiced narrative, smooth and flowing, breaks down ... I'll have to circle back to this thought some other time and place. What was it about that space?? Perhaps I can say this: the one thing I won't forget from the Finland workshop was that it was the young, unemployed chef's apprentice who spoke first, having decided it was he who knew least about whatever a 'slowlab' might be. 'What I know is this,' he said wryly, looking around at the rest of us. 'You are all from universities or have been to universities. But I know what I'm doing here.' He knew he would be cooking breakfast, lunch and dinner for us for the next four days. The rest of us were more or less suspended in the privilege of uncertainty.

Where to?

What does this chapter tell us about uncertainty as a technology? It helps us see how surrendering to process, linking with Carlin and Rendle-Short's Essaying methodology (2013) in a disruptive way, can help us move beyond what is currently known and imagine new possibilities – and these imaginings can be a confident and encouraging force that manifests collective and connected possibilities.

The structured knowing and unknowing enacted in *Essaying the FabPod* workshop offered a powerful framework through which to create new platforms for imagining, writing/essaying and documenting the possible and unknowable. It enabled us to reflect on how we might create opportunities for such collective forms of imagining – at some moments shared, at others pursued individually – and how the production of such stories of unknown futures could help us to better understand what we do not know about our lives in the continuous present. The uncertainty that animated our approach to exploring the *FabPod* allowed us to move beyond what we already knew about the structure in a way that resonates with Ingold's treatment of foresight:

> It was a matter not of *preconception* but of *anticipation*, not of determining in advance the final forms of things and all the steps needed to get there, but of

opening up a path and improvising a passage. To foresee, in this latter sense, is to see *into* the future, not to project a future state of affairs in the present; it is to look where you are going, not to fix an end-point. Such foresight is about prophecy, not prediction. And it is what enables practitioners to carry on. (Gunn and Donovan 2012: 27)

In *Essaying the FabPod*, participants were encouraged to cast forward from their past disappointments of using the *FabPod* or their current experiences of encounter to actively imagine what might coalesce next, and to continue this, step by step in conjunction with other things, humans, non-humans and in particular environments. Here, moving beyond could be considered as stepping aside of such categories that separate, to acknowledge how they in fact combine to create rich experiences. This, as intended, is also to move beyond disciplinary boundaries, as we saw in this workshop. Yet, there is another. As reflected on by David and Yoko, moving beyond, as a component of the technology of uncertainty, might be an attitude, a mindset or a specific method that we can carry forward to find opportunities to insert these into spaces and structures that may not have immediately welcomed uncertainty in the first place.

7

Propositions and Practical Applications

Figure 7.1 A movement of light traced by Simon Bowen's photograph.

In a book about uncertainty there can be no final word. However we remain sufficiently attached to the conventions of scholarship to bring together the findings of this book to advance a series of observations and propositions.

Inevitability

As we have shown through the chapters of this book, uncertainty is an inevitable element of our lives and worlds. It can bring forms of discomfort but it can also inspire and invite us to move on beyond what we thought we knew to open up new possibilities. Given the inevitability of uncertainty, we propose that it is absolutely necessary for us to be able to embrace it, whenever possible, with ways of moving forward and to build the capacity to depart from stagnant and normative practices that only perpetuate the status quo. In advocating this, we are not naively supposing that all situations of uncertainty can be embraced happily through the development of the strategies outlined in this book. Rather we are suggesting that if we are always prepared for living in forms of uncertainty that have the potential for becoming extreme enough to disrupt our existing assumptions this will enable us to fully participate in supporting people to become change-makers of their own futures. In this sense, by characterizing uncertainty as a technology, we have sought to foreground its generative potential to move us forward in productive, creative and ultimately positive ways that work to create possibility rather than preclude or limit it.

Ethics

An ethical approach to working with uncertainty is at the core of our agenda, and we propose this needs to be central to our future engagements with uncertainty. Ethics was a constant accompaniment of our workshops and over the course of the chapters, ethical considerations surfaced under various guises. This has included: the doubtful ethics of using uncertainty and precarity as a tool for generating creativity in the creative industries, particularly in the precarious affects generated by purposeful disruption; the ethics of making people feel comfortable and the importance of consensus and ownership by inviting them to opt out of activities they are not ready to participate in; the ethics of listening to participants voice their challenges, question and speak back to the facilitators; and the ethics of ensuring that participants in workshops are collaborators engaged in a learning process, rather than becoming subjects of study by the facilitators/researchers. Importantly, it also extends to the ethics of a future-focused research and change-making agenda, in which we accept that we never actually know what can happen next. This forecloses the possibility of the predictive risk mitigation of institutional ethical approval processes. Instead, a processual approach to ethics offers us ways of understanding how ethics is emergent from and part of practice as it ongoingly develops. The contexts listed above are just a start. They all figure in processes that involve uncertainty as technology because it is undertaken intentionally but also mindfully. Processes of research and intervention that engage uncertainty as a technology need to be framed with these ethical considerations in mind. We stress further that they need to be central to any intervention and change-making as it unfolds, rather than be predetermined as risk mitigation or applied retrospectively.

Collectives

Disruptions towards uncertainty, as we have shown, offer new ways to initiate and catalyse generative processes in groups, collectives, organizations, research projects and interdisciplinary investigations. We propose to nurture a culture of practitioners, equipped with an approach and orientation towards uncertainty in stepping into unknown futures together, and to invite people to participate in its making. Our workshop-based explorations of uncertainty are propositions for its role in research and creative practice. We suggest a posture or orientation towards uncertainty that treats it as generative and dynamic. Yet for uncertainty to play a generative role we need to also enable consensus around its form, use and appropriateness. As we have shown in the earlier chapters of this book there exists a range of renderings of uncertainty in existing literature across different disciplines. For it to be used as a generative technology there needs to be some agreement around the definition and use of processes related to uncertainty. We have demonstrated this through the examples of our own workshop practice. In the case of the *Temple Works* the group's collective exploration, production and decision-making came to the fore. In *Essaying the FabPod* the collective cohered through sharing individual stories. In the *Un/certainty* symposium the lunchtime makers bounced ideas and ingredients together to produce a wonderful meal. Other *Design+Ethnography+Futures* workshops not featured in this book were all co-constructed with guest facilitators who actively shaped its content, structure and possible outcomes, through which various participants cross-pollinated ideas and imagination together. That is, uncertainty was productive when it was engaged (with) collectively and consensually. When planning and developing research and intervention that uses forms of uncertainty in this way, these social, sharing and collective dimensions are significant to keep in mind.

Improvisation

A technology of uncertainty is not simply a method, a critical arm or a solution, based on our observations. Instead it awakes a process of emergence that promotes an ethics of hope, which leads to generating, collectively manifesting and sharing possibilities. It is however also a practical design that generates experience, imagination and action in the world, and that can lead to change. In the preceding chapters we have outlined the theoretical and methodological principles that inform this design, and we have shown how, in practice, designs based on uncertainty can be played out. None of these chapters has presented a clear template. Instead each of them has articulated how the ways in which uncertainty is treated as a technology and the capacity it has to disrupt, invite surrender and move beyond, which is always contingent on specific circumstances and on the improvisatory opportunities that develop in relation to these. This also means errors, misinterpretations and serendipity are willingly incorporated as a central ingredient. In this sense we do not propose a template for other researchers or practitioners to copy or follow, but rather a set of principles and examples that are intended to inspire and aid in the shaping of the use of uncertainty as a technology. This means that the principle of improvisation is at the core, not only of what we expect participants might do during workshops, but also central to the work of researchers, designers and any creative professionals who wish to facilitate workshops. As such, the interdisciplinary applications of this book are manifold: engaging with uncertainty in a workshop format is an approach that can be applied to explore any number of practical or scholarly questions, in particular those explicitly concerned with possibility, change, collectivity and richer, more expansive ways to think about the future. Indeed, it is difficult to imagine areas in which these are not ongoing matters of concern.

Emergences

Emergence has also been a central theme of this book. It was highlighted in the earlier chapters, and demonstrated through the discussions of our workshops. This theme also reflects on what is produced by projects, and in this sense we propose thinking not of 'outputs', but of how such work can continue its presence in a dynamic and ongoing way that is open to further interpretation, meaning and practice over time. Three of the workshops that we discussed included the making of digital, visual and video books, made available freely online. In each case these documents emerged from bringing together design documentation with visual ethnography into a form of blended practice. At the core of this blended practice, which tended to follow the processes and to be imbued with their effects and affects, was the concept of the trace. This means that when we think of workshops as having impact or outputs, these might not necessarily emerge in conventional or predictable forms, and might take time to gestate or become apparent. Instead it is relevant to consider how the traces of each event might best be documented and then shared, and how their different media, narratives and stories might become interwoven with each other. Moreover, it is significant to consider how to engage others in these stories, so that they join us in making traces through them, and continue to engage uncertainty as a technology to make change in the world. We have given consideration to this throughout the series and particularly so in relation to the *Un/certainty* symposium. The *Un/certainty* ebook (2015) contains multiple media that trace different elements of the event, including a series of performances that participants produced based on their experiences and collective work at the end of our encounter.

Practical applications

As we have stressed in Chapter 1, the discussions in this book have moved between the abstract and conceptual (more heavily weighted in the first three chapters) and practical examples and explorations (Chapters 4, 5 and 6). We have advocated against seeing our examples as templates or models for practice, yet we have proposed that the principle of engaging (with) and harnessing uncertainty as a generative technology can play a key role in our learning about possible futures and change-making scenarios.

The *Design+Ethnography+Futures* workshop series was exploratory and specifically focused on investigating how uncertainty might be harnessed in a generative way. In this sense the workshops we discuss here were not all part of applied research programmes in themselves. To do so would mean a possible derailing or alienation of our research partners in order to push question of uncertainty beyond their usual limits. Instead, we followed the design idea of a sandpit to 'prototype', rehearse and experiment with our approaches in contained and safe environments to be able to make mistakes, learn from breakdowns and seek continual feedback from our co-explorers, the participants. Iterating the workshops over the course of three years led to significant discoveries and insights, enabling us to share this here. Two of the workshops did have practical applications however, and here we briefly outline these and suggest their implications.

The *Essaying the FabPod* workshop formed part of a larger programme of research called *FabPod Futures*. This project brought together academic scholarship and applied practice and involved a design ethnography research project, focused on user experience of the *FabPod*, which was developed to a certain extent as a stand-alone research project that sought to understand people's biographies, perceptions and imaginations of and for the *FabPod* (Pink, Akama and Fergusson 2017). It also, in collaboration with its architect Jane Burry and acoustic engineer Xiaojun Qiu, explored ethnography in relation to research in their fields. The *Essaying the FabPod* workshop and subsequent publication played a role in this applied research activity in enabling us to garner further materials about how participants experienced the *FabPod* and how they could imagine its possible futures. Correspondences between the ways that futures were imagined in our video ethnography research and those that emerged in the stories told in the *Essaying the FabPod* iBook (2015), and the modes of making and sharing collective knowledge that David Carlin facilitated during the workshop were important in shaping our research insights. They also helped us to feed back insights into the architectural design process, which was ongoing into the design of a new *FabPod* prototype in the following year.

The *Un/certainty* symposium was on the one hand an experimental event, yet it also served to respond to some of the core questions that Yoko and Sarah had been confronting in relation to our interests in bringing together design and ethnography as a form of blended practice (Pink, Akama and Fergusson 2017). The two-day symposium indeed shed light on a range of issues. However one of those most pertinent to our investigation was what it taught us about the relationship between ethnography and design, and the place of uncertainty in each practice. As discussed elsewhere (*Un/certainty* 2015) we learnt that uncertainty sits differently in design and ethnography, in that although it was considered to be central to both practices, it has a different place and relevance in the conventional practice and temporalities of each. This highlighted a key issue that not only helped us to understand differences between the participants in the symposium, but also one that needs to be accounted for in future interdisciplinary work that seeks to make correspondences between the two disciplines.

Since completing the *Design+Ethnography+Futures* exploratory workshop series, both Yoko and Sarah have applied principles and insights from this work in a range of different contexts that have specifically engaged with real-world problems. These include Sarah's collaborative *Creative Health/Salud Creativa* project and Yoko's work with Australian Indigenous nations to strategize self-determination in the absence of formal nation recognition by the government.

Sarah has been working with the anthropologist of health Ana Martínez Pérez (Ecuador) and the artist and poet Florentino Díaz (Peru) with whom Sarah developed a three-day workshop in Quito (Ecuador) bringing design anthropology principles together with ethnographies of health contexts in Ecuador and creative practice. This workshop sought to develop ways of conceptualizing issues around public, crisis and rural health through an awareness of how contingency, improvisation and creativity shape health in practice, and a focus on how we might create possibilities rather than solutions as we move into uncertain terrain. Thus one of the aims was to go beyond existing ways of thinking about these problems in a structured but generative and creative mode. However in this applied research context, the aim was not to develop a disruptive or difficult mode of departure or uncertainty but rather to find meaningful ways in which to understand how uncertainty figured in the processes that were involved. This work is now being developed into an experimental handmade book, as well as the *Salud Creativa* book (being developed by Martínez Pérez, Pink and Díaz).

Yoko's research collaboration with her Indigenous partners ran in parallel to the *Design+Ethnography+Futures* programme, and as such, uncertainty as disruption, surrender and moving beyond weaved throughout, crystallizing and manifesting in her applied research in various ways. Disruption is most acutely felt and enacted to challenge Australia's colonial history and current policies that focus on Indigenous disadvantage in a political movement by attending to the consciousness of Indigenous sovereignty. As a researcher and a resident sharing, living and working on Indigenous land, this means carving out ways to design a meeting place of multiple sovereigns through various Indigenous-led events, gatherings and engagements (see Akama et al. 2017). This necessitated an unlearning of certain framings of design, like its over-reliance on strategies, models, methods and tools to 'solve problems', and surrender constructs that only recognize change in the visible and the vocal (Akama 2018). Embracing uncertainty enabled Yoko to incorporate silence, ambiguity and serendipity as a significant component of change and transformation. And while designing various mechanisms for Indigenous participation to promote necessary discussions on self-governance and cultural renewal, Yoko is also undergoing cultural renewal of her own Japanese heritage to foreground respect, reciprocity and interrelatedness to move beyond together, with her Indigenous friends and collaborators, towards futures built upon mutually respectful sovereign relationships.

* * *

If we believe that what we do with people matters, we need to acknowledge that how, when and whom our collaborations impact on, or why this happens, is impossible to know before we intervene. This should not however deter us from working with partners in research and design towards change-making. It is our hope that this book can be considered as a gift and an encouragement to embrace a living paradox called uncertainty.

References

Adey, P. and Anderson, B. (2011), 'Affect and Security: Exercising Emergency in UK Civil Contingencies', *Environment and Planning D: Society and Space*, 29: 1092–1109.

Akama, Y. (2015), 'Being Awake to Ma: Designing in Between-ness as a Way of Becoming With', *Co-Design: International Journal of CoCreation in Design and the Arts*, 11(3–4): 262–74.

Akama, Y. (2015), 'Continuous Re-Configuring of Invisible Social Structures', in A. Bruni, L. L. Parolin and C. Schubert (eds), *Designing Technology Work Organization and Vice Versa*, 163–83. Wilmington, US: Vernon Press.

Akama, Y. (2018), 'Surrendering to the Ocean: Practices of Mindfulness and Presence in Designing', in R. B. Egenhoefer (ed.), *The Routledge Handbook of Sustainable Design*, 219–30. London and New York: Routledge.

Akama, Y. and Light, A. (2012), 'A Candour in Reporting: Designing Dexterously for Fire Preparedness', in Proceedings of CHI 2012, ACM Digital Library: 281–90.

Akama, Y. and Prendiville, A. (2013), 'Embodying, Enacting and Entangling Design: A Phenomenological View to Co-designing Services', *Swedish Design Research Journal*, (1): 29–40.

Akama, Y., Pink, S. and Fergusson, A. (2015), 'Design + Ethnography + Futures: Surrendering in Uncertainty', in the proceedings of CHI '15 Extended Abstract, ACM Digital Library: 531–42.

Akama, Y., Stuedahl, D. and Zyl, I. V. (2015), 'Design Disruptions in Contested, Contingent and Contradictory Future-Making', *Interaction Design and Architecture Journal*, 26: 132–48.

Akama, Y., Moline, K. and Pink, S. (2016), 'Disruptive Interventions with Mobile media Through Design+Ethnography+Futures', in L. Hjorth, H. Horst, A. Galloway and G. Bell (eds), *Companion to Digital Ethnography*, 458–69. London and New York: Routledge.

Akama, Y., Chaplin, S., Philips, R. and Toh, K. (2012), 'Design-led Strategies for Bushfire Preparedness', in Proceedings of Earth: Fire and Rain – Australian & New Zealand Disaster and Emergency Management Conference: 407–24.

Akama, Y., Evans, D., Keen, S., McMillan, F., McMillan, M. and West, P. (2017), 'Designing Digital and Creative Scaffolds to Strengthen Indigenous Nations: Being

Waradjuri by Practising Sovereignty', *Journal of Digital Creativity*, 28(1) (Special Issue on Digital Citizenship), 58–72. doi:10.1080/14626268.2017.1291525

Amin, A. (2013), 'Surviving the Turbulent Future', *Environment and Planning D: Society and Space*, 31: 140–56.

Amit, V. (2000), 'The University as Panopticon: Moral Claims and Attacks on Academic Freedom', in M. Strathern (ed.), *Audit Cultures: Anthropological Studies in Accountability*, 215–35. London: Routledge.

Anderson, R. (2016), 'The Rashomon Effect and Communication', *Canadian Journal of Communication*, 41(2): 249–69.

Anusas, M. and Harkness, R. (2016), 'Different Presents in the Making', in R. C. Smith, K. T. Vangkilde, M. G. Kjærsgaard, T. Otto, J. Halse and T. Binder (eds), *Design Anthropological Futures*, 55–70. London: Bloomsbury Academic.

Balducci, A., Boelens, L., Hillier, J., Nyseth, T. and Wilkinson, C. (2011), 'Strategic Spatial Planning in Uncertainty: Theory and Exploratory Practice', *Town Planning Review*, 82(5): 481–501.

Bauman, Z. (2007), *Liquid Times: Living in an Age of Uncertainty*. Cambridge: Polity Press.

Beck, U. (1994), 'The Reinvention of Politics', in U. Beck, A. Giddens, and S. Lash (eds), *Reflexive Modernization: Politics, Tradition and Aesthetics in the Modern Social Order*, 1–55. Stanford: Stanford University Press.

Beck, U. (2006), 'Living in the World Risk Society', *Economy and Society*, 35(3): 329–45.

Bell, G., Blythe, M. and Sengers, P. (2005), 'Making by Making Strange: Defamiliarization and the Design of Domestic Technologies', *ACM Transactions Human Computer Interactions*, 12(2): 149–73.

Berg, M. and Fors, V. (2017), 'Workshops as Nodes of Knowledge Co-production: Beyond ideas of Automagical Synergies', in S. Pink, V. Fors and T. O'Dell (eds), *Theoretical Scholarship and Applied Practice*, 53–72. Oxford: Berghahn.

Bergvall-Kåreborn, B., Eriksson, C. I., Ståhlbröst, A. and Svensson, J., eds (2009), *A Milieu for Innovation: Defining Living Labs*. ISPIM Innovation Symposium, 6–9 December 2009.

Binder, T. (2016), 'The Things we do: Encountering the Possible', in R. C. Smith, K. T. Vangkilde, M. G. Kjærsgaard, T. Otto, J. Halse and T. Binder (eds), *Design Anthropological Futures*, 267–81. London: Bloomsbury Academic.

Bissell, D. (2010), 'Passenger Mobilities: Affective Atmospheres and the Sociality of Public Transport', *Environment and Planning D: Society and Space*, 28: 270–89.

Bødker, S. and Grønbæk, K. (1991), 'Cooperative Prototyping: Users and Designers in Mutual Activity', *International Journal of Man-Machine Studies – Computer-supported Cooperative Work and Groupware*, 34(3): 453–78.

Bogost, I. (2012), *Alien Phenomenology, or, what it's Like to be a Thing*. Minneapolis: University of Minnesota Press.

Borraz, O. (2011), 'From Risk to the Government of Uncertainty: The Case of Mobile Telephony', *Journal of Risk Research*, 14(8): 969–82.

Bresland, J. (2014), 'On the Origin of the Video Essay', *Blackbird: An Online Journal of Literature and the Arts*, 9(1).

Cappello, M. (2013), 'Propositions; Provocations: Inventions', in M. Singer and N. Walker (eds), *Bending Genre*, 65–75. New York: Bloomsbury.

Carlin, D. (2017), 'The Essay in the Anthropocene: Towards Entangled Nonfiction', *TEXT Journal Of Writing And Writing Courses*, 21(1): 38.

Carlin, D. and Rendle-Short F. (2013), 'Nonfiction Now: A (non)introduction', *TEXT Journal Of Writing And Writing Courses*, 17(2): 18.

Carlin, D. and Rendle-Short, F. (2016), 'In the Company of: Composing a Collaborative Residency Programme for Writers', *New Writing: The International Journal for the Practice and Theory of Creative Writing*, 21 July. Available online: http://www.tandfonline.com/doi/full/10.1080/14790726.2016.1203956 (accessed 30 July 2016).

Carlin, D., Akama, Y., Pink, S., Miles, A., Brettle, K., Fergusson, A., Magner, B., Pang, A., Rendle-Short, F. and Sumartojo, S. (2015), 'Essaying The Fabpod: An Improvised Experimental Collaborative Account of the Uncertain Cultural Life and Futures of the Fabpod, as of August 21, 2014', *Axon Journal*, 8. Available online: http://www.axonjournal.com.au/issue-8-1/essaying-fabpod (accessed 24 May 2016).

Cefkin, M., ed. (2009), *Ethnography and the Corporate Encounter*. Oxford: Berghahn.

Conradson, D. and Latham, A. (2007), 'The Affective Possibilities of London: Antipodean Transnationals and the Overseas Experience', *Mobilities*, 2(2): 231–54.

Design Council (n.d.) 'Five Top Tips to Run a Successful Design Workshop'. Available online: http://www.designcouncil.org.uk/news-opinion/five-top-tips-run-successful-design-workshop (accessed on 4th June 2017).

Dunne, A. and Raby, F. (2001), *Design Noir: The Secret Life of Electronic Objects*. Basel: Birkhäuser.

Dunne, A. and Raby, F. (2013), *Speculative Everything: Design, Fiction, and Social Dreaming*. Cambridge, MA: The MIT Press.

Edensor, T. (2007), 'Sensing the Ruin', *The Senses and Society*, 2(2): 217–22.

Essaying the FabPod: An improvised experimental collaborative account of the uncertain cultural life and futures of the fabpod as of August 21 2014 (2014), ed. A. Miles and D. Carlin. Available online: http://vogmae.net.au/works/2014/rezine02.ibooks (accessed 30 December 2014).

Fry, T. (2009), *Design Futuring: Sustainability, Ethics and New Practice*. Oxford, UK: Berg.

Galloway, A. (2007), 'Seams and Scars, Or How to Locate Accountability in Collaborative Work', in C. Brickwood, B. Ferran, D. Garcia and T. Putnam (eds), *(un)common Ground: Creative Encounters across Sectors and Disciplines*, 152–8. Amsterdam: BIS Publishers.

Garfinkel, H. (1967), *Studies in Ethnomethodology*. Englewood Cliffs, NJ: Prentice-Hall.

Gatt, C. and Ingold, T. (2013), 'From Description to Correspondence: Anthropology in Real Time', in W. Gunn, T. Otto and R. Charlotte-Smith (eds), *Design Anthropology*, 139–58. New York: Bloomsbury.

Gaver, W., Beaver, J. and Benford, S. (2003), 'Ambiguity as a Resource for Design', CHI 2003 proceedings: 233–40.

Giddens, A. (1999), 'Risk and Responsibility', *The Modern Law Review*, 62(1): 1–10.

Goldstein, J. (1999), 'Emergence as a Construct: History and Issues', *Emergence*, 1(1): 49–73.

Goodman, E., Stolterman, E. and Wakkary, R. (2011), 'Understanding Interaction Design Practices', in Proceedings of CHI 2011, ACM Digital Library: 1061–70.

Green, J. (2009), 'Is it Time for the Sociology of Health to Abandon "Risk"?' *Health, Risk & Society*, 11(6): 493–508.

Gunn, S. and Hillier, J. (2014), 'When Uncertainty is Interpreted as Risk: An Analysis of Tensions Relating to Spatial Planning Reform in England', *Planning Practice & Research*, 29(1): 56–74.

Gunn, W. and Donovan, J., eds (2012), *Design and Anthropology*. Farnham: Ashgate.

Gunn, W., Otto, T. and Smith, R. C., eds (2013), *Design Anthropology: Theory and Practice*. London and New York: Bloomsbury.

Halse, J. (2013), 'Ethnographies of the Possible', in W. Gunn, T. Otto and R. C. Smith (eds), *Design Anthropology: Theory and Practice*, 180– 96. London and New York: Bloomsbury.

Halse, J and Boffi, L. (2016) 'Design Interventions as a Form of Inquiry', in R. C. Smith, K. T. Vangkilde, M. G. Kjærsgaard, T. Otto, J. Halse and T. Binder (eds), *Design Anthropological Futures*, 89–104. London: Bloomsbury Academic.

Haraway, D. J. (2008), *When Species Meet*. Minneapolis and London: University of Minnesota Press.

Ingold, T. (1993), 'Temporality of Landscape', *World Archaeology*, 25(2): 152–74.

Ingold, T. (2012), 'Introduction: The Perception of the User-producer', in W. Gunn and J. Donovan (eds), *Design and Anthropology*, 19–33. Ashgate: Farnham.

Ingold, T. (2013), *Making: Anthropology, Archaeology, Art and Architecture*. Abingdon, UK: Routledge.

Kasulis, T. (2002), *Intimacy or Integrity: Philosophical and Cultural Difference*. Hawaii: University of Hawaii Press.

Kjærsgaard, M. G., Halse, J., Smith, R. C., Vangkilde, K. T., Binder, T. and Otto, T. (2016), 'Introduction: Design Anthropological Futures', in R. C. Smith, K. T. Vangkilde, M. G. Kjærsgaard, T. Otto, J. Halse and T. Binder (eds), *Design Anthropological Futures*, 1–16. London: Bloomsbury Academic.

Lane Kauffmann, R. (1988), 'The Skewed Path: Essaying as Un-methodical Method', *Diogenes*, 36(143): 66–92.

Latour, B. (2005), *Reassembling the Social: An Introduction to Actor-Network-Theory*. Oxford: Oxford University Press.

Latour, B. (2008), 'Powers of the Facsimile: A Turing Test on Science and Literature', in S. J. Burn and P. Dempsey (eds), *Intersections: Essays on Richard Powers*, 263–92. Urbana-Champaign, IL: Archive Press.

Law, J. (2004), *After Method: Mess in Social Science Research*. London: Routledge.

Lawson, B. (2004), *What Designers Know*. Oxford: Elsevier.

Lewis, S. and Gallant, A. (2013), 'In Science, the Only Certainty is Uncertainty', *The Conversation*, 22 August. Available online: https://theconversation.com/in-science-the-only-certainty-is-uncertainty-17180 (accessed 1 September 2015).

Light, A. (2011), 'HCI as Heterodoxy: Technologies of Identity and the Queering of Interaction with Computers', *Interacting with Computers*, 23: 430–8.

Light, A. (2015), 'Troubling Futures: Can Participatory Design Research Provide a Constitutive Anthropology for the 21st Century?' *Interaction Design and Architecture(s) Journal*, (26): 81–94.

Light, A. and Akama, Y. (2012), 'The Human Touch: From Method to Participatory Practice in Facilitating Design with Communities', in Proceedings of PDC' 12, ACM Digital Library: 61–70.

Light, A. and Akama, Y. (2014), 'Structuring Future Social Relations: The Politics of Care in Participatory Practice', in Proceedings PDC 2014, ACM Digital Library: 151–60.

Lopate, P. (1995), *The Art of the Personal Essay*. New York: Anchor Books.

Lupton, D. (2013), 'Risk and Emotion: Towards an Alternative Theoretical Perspective', *Health, Risk & Society*, 15(8): 634–47.

Lupton, D. (2013), *Risk*. London: Routledge.

Martínez Pérez, A., Pink, S. and Díaz, F. (2018), *Salud Creativa*. Quito: Universidad de las Américas (forthcoming).

Maurer, B. (2005), 'Introduction: Ethnographic Emergences', *American Anthropologist*, 107(2): 1–4.

Mccarthy, E. (2010), *Ethics Embodied: Rethinking Selfhood through Continental, Japanese and Feminist Philosophies*. Lanham, MD: Lexington Books.

Michael, M. (2012), 'De-signing the Object of Sociology: Toward an "Idiogic" Methodology', *The Sociological Review*, 60(1): 166–83.

Miyazaki, H. (2004), *The Method of Hope: Anthropology, Philosophy and Fijian Knowledge*. Stanford, CA: Stanford University Press.

Moline, K. (2012), 'The Relationship Between Experimental Design and the Artistic Avant-Gardes (1998–2007)', PhD Dissertation, School of Art & Design, University of New South Wales, Sydney.

Moline, K. (2015), 'Myths of the Near Future 2: Equipment', in K. Moline and P. Hall (eds), *Experimental Thinking/Design Practices*, Griffith University Art Gallery.

Montaigne, M. (1993), *The Complete Essays*. London: Penguin Classics.

Moran, T. P. (2002), 'Everyday Adaptive Design', in Proceedings of DIS 2002, ACM Digital Library: 13–14.

Morgan, J. and Pink, S. (2017), 'Researcher Safety? Ethnography in the Interdisciplinary World of Audit Cultures', *Cultural Studies ↔ Critical Methodologies*.

Morton, T., Rabinovich, A., Marshall, D. and Bretschneider, P. (2011), 'The Future that may (or may not) Come: How Framing Changes Responses to Uncertainty in Climate Change Communications', *Global Environmental Change*, 21: 103–9.

Murphy, K. and Marcus, G. (2013), 'Epilogue: Ethnography and Design, Ethnography in Design, Ethnography by Design', in W. Gunn, T. Otto and R. C. Smith (eds), *Design Anthropology. Theory and Practice*, 251–68. London and New York: Bloomsbury.

Nancy, J.-L. (2000), *Being Singular Plural*. Translated by R. D. Richardson and A. E. O'Byrne. Stanford, CA: Stanford University Press.

Pellizzoni, L. (2003), 'Knowledge, Uncertainty and the Transformation of the Public Sphere', *European Journal of Social Theory*, 6(3): 327–55.

Pels, P. (2000), 'The Trickster's Dilemma: Ethics and the Technologies of the Anthropological Self', in M. Strathern (ed.), *Audit Cultures: Anthropological Studies in Accountability*, 135–72. London: Routledge.

Pink, S. (2011), 'Drawing with Our Feet (and trampling the maps): Walking with Video as a Graphic anthropology', in T. Ingold (ed.), *Redrawing Anthropology*, 143–56. Farnham: Ashgate.

Pink, S. (2013), *Doing Visual Ethnography*. London: Sage.

Pink, S. and Leder Mackley, K. (2012), 'Video as a Route to Sensing Invisible Energy', *Sociological Research Online*, February. Available online: http://www.socresonline.org.uk/17/1/3.html

Pink, S., Morgan, J. and Dainty, A. (2015), 'Other People's Homes as Sites of Uncertainty: Ways of Knowing and Being Safe', *Environment and Planning A* 47(2): 450–64.

Pink, S., Lingard, H. and Harley, J. (2017), 'Refiguring Creativity in Virtual Work: The Digital-Material Construction Site', *New Technology, Work and Employment*, 32(1): 12–27.

Pink, S., Akama, Y. and Fergusson, A. (2017), 'Researching Future as an Alterity of the Present', in J. F. Salazar, S. Pink, A. Irving and J. Sjöberg (eds), *Anthropologies and Futures: Researching Emerging and Uncertain Worlds*, 133–50. London and New York: Bloomsbury.

Rendell, J. (2013), 'A Way with Words: Feminists Writing Architectural Design Research', in M. Fraser (ed.), *Architectural Design Research*, 117–36. London: Ashgate.

Rendle-Short, F. (2015), 'How the How: The Question of Form in Writing Creative Scholarly Works', *New Writing*, 12(1): 91–100.

Rockström, J. (2009), 'A Safe Operating Space for Humanity', *Nature* 461: 472–5. Available online: http://www.nature.com/nature/journal/v461/n7263/full/461472a.html (accessed 20 August 2015).

Rose, D. B. (2004), *Reports from a Wild Country: Ethics for Decolonisation*. Sydney: University of New South Wales.

Rosenberg, T. (2006), 'Designs on Critical Practice?' in Proceedings of Reflections on Creativity Conference.

Salazar, J. F., Pink, S., Irving, A. and Sjöberg, J., eds (2017), *Anthropologies and Futures: Researching Emerging and Uncertain Worlds*. London: Bloomsbury.

Samimian-Darash, L. and Rabinow, P., eds (2015), *Modes of Uncertainty: Anthropological Cases*. Chicago: University of Chicago Press.

Sanders, E. B. (2002), 'Scaffolds for Experiencing in the New Design Space', in Institute for Information Design Japan (ed.), *Information Design*, 1–6. IID.J, Graphic-Sha Publishing, 1–6. Available online: http://www.maketools.com/articles-papers/ScaffoldsforExperiencing_Sanders_03.pdf (accessed 23 October 2007).

Schön, D. (1983), *The Reflective Practitioner: How Professionals Think in Action*. New York: Basic Books.

Sennett, R. (2008), *The Craftsman*. London: Penguin.

Sennett, R. (2012), *Together*. London: Penguin.

Shields, D. (2010), *Reality Hunger*. New York: Alfred A Knopf.

Simon, H. A. (1968), *The Sciences of the Artificial*. Cambridge, MA: MIT Press.

Simone, H. A. (2013), 'Cities of Uncertainty: Jakarta, the Urban Majority, and Inventive Political Technologies', *Theory Culture & Society*, 30(7/8): 243–63.

Smith, R. C. and Otto, T. (2016), 'Cultures of the Future: Emergence and Intervention in Design Anthropology', in R. C. Smith, K. T. Vangkilde, M. G. Kjærsgaard, T.

Otto, J. Halse and T. Binder (eds), *Design Anthropological Futures*, 19–36. London: Bloomsbury Academic.

Smith, R. C., Vangkilde, K. T., Kjærsgaard, M. G., Otto, T., Halse, J. and Binder, T., eds (2016), *Design Anthropological Futures*. London: Bloomsbury Academic.

Sneath, D., Holbraad, M. and Pedersen, M. (2009), 'Technologies of the Imagination: An Introduction', *Ethnos*, 74(1): 5–30.

Solnit, R. (2016), *Hope in the Dark: Untold Histories, Wild Possibilities*. Edinburgh: Cannongate Books.

Sperschneider, W. (2007), 'Video Ethnography Under Industrial Constraints: Observational Techniques and Video analysis', in S. Pink (ed.), *Visual Interventions*, 273–94. Oxford: Berghahn.

Stewart, K. (2010), 'Atmospheric Attunements', *Rubric*, 1: 1–14. Available online: http://rubric.org.au/wp-content/uploads/2010/05/Atmospheric-Attunements.pdf (accessed 30 April 2017).

Stewart, K. (2012), 'Precarity's Forms', *Cultural Anthropology*, 27(3): 518–25.

Storni, C. (2012), 'Unpacking Design Practices: The Notion of Thing in the Making of Artifacts', *Science, Technology & Human Values*, 37(1): 88–123.

Storni, C. (2014), 'The Problem of De-sign as Conjuring: Empowerment-in-use and the Politics of Seams', paper presented to Participatory Design Conference, Windhoek, Namibia.

Strathern, M. (2000), 'Afterword: Accountability … and Ethnography', in M. Strathern (ed.), *Audit Cultures: Anthropological Studies in Accountability*, 279–304. London: Routledge.

Suchman, L. (2002), 'Located Accountabilities in Technology Production', *Scandinavian Journal of Information Systems*, 12(2): 91–105.

Sumartojo, S. (2014), 'Dazzling Relief: Floodlighting and National Affective Atmospheres on VE Day 1945', *Journal of Historical Geography*, 45: 59–69.

Tall, D. and D'Agata, J. (1997), 'The Lyric Essay', *Seneca Review*(Fall). Available online: http://www.hws.edu/academics/senecareview/lyricessay.aspx (accessed 25 November 2016).

Temple Works (2015), 'Uncertainty at Temple Works, Leeds', 22 June 2015. Available online: https://issuu.com/templeworks/docs/temple_works_2015 (accessed 30 July 2016).

Tierney, K. (2015), 'Resilience and the Neoliberal Project: Discourses, Critiques, Practices – And Katrina', *American Behavioral Scientist*, 59(10): 1327–42.

Tulloch, J. and Lupton, D. (2003), *Risk and Everyday Life*. London: Sage.

Un/certainty (2015), ed. S. Pink and Y. Akama. Available online: http://d-e-futures.com/projects/uncertainty/ (accessed 30 January 2015).

Varela, F. J., Thompson, E. and Rosch, E. (1993), *The Embodied Mind: Cognitive Science and Human Experience*. Cambridge, MA: MIT Press.

Watts, L., Ehn, P. and Suchman, L. (2014), 'Prologue', in P. Ehn, E. M. Nilsson and R. Topgaard (eds), *Making Futures: Marginal Notes on Innovation, Design, and Democracy*, ix–xxxix. Cambridge, MA: MIT Press.

Williams, N., Cherrey, J., Peters, B. and Burry, J. (2013), 'FabPod: A Prototypical Design System for Acoustically Diffused Enclosures', in M. Stacey (ed.), *Prototyping Architecture: The Conference Papers*. London: Building Centre Trust.

Zeiderman, A., Ahmad Kaker, S., Silver, J. and Wood, A. (2015), 'Uncertainty and Urban Life', *Public Culture*, 27(2). Available online: doi: 10.1215/08992363-2841868

Index

action, uncertainty as technology of   45–8
   DIY maker-culture impact   47
   'seams and scars' to users   47–8
Actor Network Theory   6
affective charge   118
affirmative design   100
affordance of uncertainty   13, 43–4, 103
   disruption (*see* disruption, uncertainty as technology for)
   moving beyond   103
      (*see also* moving beyond)
   of technologies   45, 48
   way of conceptualizing   29
anthropological ethnography   6, 49
anthropological literatures   37
anthropological mode of uncertainty   34
anthropology   1, 6, 11, 13, 19, 41, 103
   constitutive anthropology   49
   corporate anthropology   12
   of design   63
   design anthropology
      (*see* design anthropology)
   technologies   26
'anthropology at home' movement   49
apocalyptic moment   1
appropriation   44
attending to uncertainty   9, 47, 119
attuning   6, 47, 119

'becoming with'   11, 47, 62
Berg, Martin (Swedish scholar in sociology)   71
brief-but-vivid narratives   7, 104

cause-and-effect   3
change   5, 6, 81
   attending to uncertainty   9
   driven by neoliberal capitalism   21
   organizational change   27
   purposeful change   53
   social change   21
   socio-cultural change   44

   and uncertainty   10, 42, 129
   unexpected and serendipitous   50, 132
change-makers   2, 125
change-making   2–5, 8, 17, 19, 23, 30, 42–3, 46, 56–7
   to build capacity   82
   forms of   23
   learning about   130
   processes   30
   processual modes of   81
   uncertain approaches to   77, 79, 82
chaos theory   24
climate science   24
   process of climate change communication   24
   specialist technical knowledge   31
co-designing   4, 7, 12
   literatures   37
collective essaying   117
collectives   18, 127–8
   appropriateness   127
   Design+Ethnography+Futures workshop   127
   Essaying the FabPod workshop   127
   sharing   128
   Temple Works workshop   127
   Un/certainty symposium   127
competitive gambling   28
conceptualization of uncertainty   26, 32, 46
confidence   32, 77, 85, 101
constitutive anthropology   11, 49
contemporary (dis)alignments   60–3
   attitude   62
   becoming with   62
   design anthropology   61
   Design+Ethnography+Futures research programme   60, 62
   disrupting echoes   61
   inter- or trans-disciplinary movements   61
   interrogation   63

contradictory emotions 82
control and uncertainty 90–3
  collaborative activity 90
  degrees of willingness to surrender 91
  new ideas of uncertainty 91
  normative structure 91
  orientating structure 91
  overpowering embodiment 91
  risk-averse 91
  sensory deprivation 90
Creative Health/Salud Creativa project 131
creative practice research 4
creative uncertainty 27
criticisms 10, 22
cultural renewal 132

design 10, 103
  ethnography research project 130
  intentions 118
  practical design 128
design anthropology 4, 6, 12–13, 49, 131
  intention to disrupt 61
  need to surrender 52
  principles of emergence and intervention 13
  'third spaces' 14
design documentation 13, 129
  from *Mindfulness and Technology* workshop 14
design interventions 9, 118
design laboratory 14
Design+Ethnography+Futures workshop 2, 11, 41, 48, 51, 54, 60, 62, 70, 77, 131, 132
  collaborative practice as cat's cradle 4
  safe environments 130
dialogues about possibility 9
discovering capacity 97–9
  accompanying the change 98
  capacity to surrender 99
  Design+Ethnography+Futures series 99
  generative forms of uncertainty 98
  interrelatedness of elements 97
  locating enjoyment 98
  precarious conditions 97
  process of collective exploration 97
disempowerment 52, 77
disruption 15, 17–18, 132

disruption as destructive force, ethnographies of lunch 75–8
  ethical dilemma 78
  generative possibilities 76
  minimal group momentum 75
  need for creativity 76
  positive outcome 75
  principles of good ethnography 77
  reflexive approach 78–9
  self-reflexive interrogations 76
  tyranny of uncertainty 77
  unexpected uncertainty 78
disruption as generative catalyst, lunch-making task 73–5
  disrupting conventional approaches 75
  eating and sharing 74
  elaborate techniques, inventions 74
disruption strategies 59
  considering uncertainty through disruption 78–9
  contemporary (dis)alignments 60–3
  as destructive force 75–8
  of everyday technology norms 66–9
  as generative catalyst 73–5
  hungry digital ghost 60
  making as disruption 63–6
  structuring tension and balance 70–3
disruption, uncertainty as technology for 48–51
  anthropological ethnography 49
  'anthropology at home' movement 48
  constitutive anthropology 49
  Critical Design 50
  ethnographic sensibility 49
  forms of disruption 51
  Placebo objects 50
  processes of defamiliarization 48
  revised ethnographic approach and sensibility 49
  Speculative Design 50
documentation 117, 129

embeddedness 118
emergence and modes of engagement 4–9
  creative writing 7
  design anthropology 6
  moving beyond 5, 7

notions of emergence(s)   5, 18, 129
photographic ethnography   8, 9
video ethnography techniques   7–9
enterprise uncertainty   28
erosion of oppositional categories   82
essaying methodology   110–11
   creative non-fiction   111
   FabPod essaying workshop   111
   lyric essay   110
   technique of 'essaying'   110
   video essay   110
Essaying the FabPod workshop   7, 16, 77, 103, 105–6, 130
   design ethnography   130
   essaying methodology   110–11
   methods   111–17
   moving beyond   117–22
   where to   122–3
   why *FabPod*   107–9
Essaying the FabPod workshop, methods   111–17
   improvisations   116
   integrity and intimacy-oriented   117
   knowing and heuristics   116–17
   knowledge   117
   Method 1, arranged in line   111–13
   Method 2, knowledge circle   113–15
   Method 3, data assemblage   115
   Method 4, writing   115
   Method 5, being-alongside   115
   Method 6, a second flash-essay   115
   Method 7, sharing   115
   new ways of thinking   116
   sharing   117
   spectrum of uncertainty   111
   symmetrical halves   111
ethics   18, 126–7
   risk mitigation   127
ethnographic sensibility   49
everyday technology norms, disrupting of   66–9
   benefits of   68
   discomfort in openness   67
   disruptive research explorations   67
   generating thematic insights   68–9
   image-making algorithm   68
   'permission' to strangers for accessing   67
   personal and collective surrender   68
   swap phones suggestions   66
   video-making process   69
'exaptation'   44
experience, uncertainty as technology of   45–8
   human–computer Interaction   47
   'seams and scars' to users   47–8
expertise   31
   conceptualization of   32

FabPod   51, 56, 105–6, 130
   ambitious experiment   107
   essaying methodology   110–11
   Essaying the FabPod workshop   108
   interior environment   108
   meeting space   109
   object for *Design+Ethnography+Futures* workshop   108
   re-imagining   108
   RMIT's Design Hub building   107
   surrender in play in   53
ficto-critical writing   104
forms of uncertainty   21, 27–30, 41
   destructive forms of   59
   generative forms of   60, 70, 98
   living in   125, 128
   making of   99
framings of design   132
further thinking   57
future-making   1, 5, 11, 100–1

hands-on-doing   12
hidden dimensions   2
Human–Computer Interaction   47, 109

imagination, uncertainty as technology of   45–8
   definition   46
   indeterminate outcome   47
improvisation   18, 35, 116, 128
inevitability   18, 23, 51, 125
innovation   12, 26, 28, 33, 64
intentional engaging   39
intervention   9
invocations   71–2
   collection of musings   72
   lunch-making activity   72–3

Index

knowledge 91, 117
   expert knowledge 33
   'lay' or 'anecdotal' knowledge 31–2
   legitimate knowledge 31
   proprietary knowledge 47
   technical knowledge 31
knowledge production 17, 32

learning through doing 34
learning through hands-on-doing 12
learning through unlearning 81
Living Labs (collaborative space) 15
locating uncertainty 87–90
   anxiety 88
   disappointment 89
   discomfort to adventure 87
   human-chain snaking 88
   imagination 88
   Rashomon Effect 88
   singular truth 89
   temporary illusion 89

making as disruption 63–6
   creative spaces 63
   idea of sensemaking 64
   process of the workshop 64
   rehearsal 65
   reshaping and refining the concepts 65
   Spaces of Innovation workshop 63
   video-making process 66
   video recording 65
material making 40, 64
messiness of research 42
misapprehension 82, 94
misinterpretation 82, 128
   discomfort in openness 67
   disruptive research explorations 37
   'permission' to strangers for accessing 67
movement of light 94, 126
moving beyond
   affective charge 118
   approach to emergence 103
   atmospheric attunements 119
   collective essaying 117
   creating rich experiences 123
   documentation 117
   embeddedness 118
   matters of concern 104
   matters of facts 104
   non-fiction creative writing 105–6
   parody of certainty 104
   purposefulness 118
   reflections 121–2
   shifting perceptions 120
   thoughts 120–1
   treatment of foresight 122–3
   visual documentation 118
moving beyond, uncertainty as technology for 5, 15, 54–6
   carrying responsibilities 55
   for generation of possibility 54
   philosophies of human 55
   re-engaging 55
   resources of knowledge 56
Myths of the Near Future workshop 17, 51, 56, 66, 69, 79
   video documentation process 69

non-fiction creative writing 105–6
   disruption and surrender 106
   FabPod 105
   risky accounts 105

objects of analysis 40
Occupational Safety and Health (OSH) measures 85
online gambling 36
openness, risk of 54

Participatory Design discourses 108
photographic ethnography 8, 9
politics of uncertainty 30–3
   body and mind 30
   concomitant legitimacy 33
   expertise 31, 32, 33
   knowledge production 32
   radical uncertainty 32
   risk related to perception 31
   uncertainty as generative 33
practical applications 129–32
preparing stage, of uncertainty 83–7
   anticipatory affects 84
   anticipatory logics 85
   audit cultures 85
   'managing' uncertainty 85
   regulatory regimes of neoliberal societies 85
   snippets of eavesdropping 86

productive ambiguity   97
propositions
    collectives   127–8
    emergences   129
    ethics   126–7
    improvisation   128
    inevitability   125
    movement of light   126
purposefulness   118

Rashomon Effect   88
re-figuring, uncertainty as technology for   43–5
    affordances of technologies   45
    concept of 'exaptation'   44
    concept of technology   43
    notion of 'appropriation'   44
    refinement   44
    socio-cultural situations   44
    technologies of the imagination   43–4
resilience   25
rethinking of things   40
risk   22
    decentring risk   23
    insistence   23
    and uncertainty   23

self-governance   132
sense of optimism   101
sociological literatures   37
sovereign relationships   132
Spaces of Innovation workshop   8, 17, 51, 63–5, 68, 79
spaciousness of uncertainty   3
Spatial Information Architecture Laboratory (SIAL)   107
structuring tension and balance   70–3
    frustration and enjoyment   72
    invocations   71–2
    setting hierarchies   70
    time-poor academics   72
    workshops   70, 71
surrender, uncertainty as technology for   15, 17, 51–4, 81, 96
    acts of unlearning   52
    change-making   52
    co-ontological approach   52
    disempowerment   52
    need to surrender   53

openness, risk of   54
precariousness and creativity   53
to test the limits of willingness   53

technologies of the imagination   40, 43–4
Temple Works workshop   16, 53, 77, 83
    creative expression   92
    industrial ruin   92
    preparing   83–7
    tracing (*see* tracing stage, of uncertainty)
    trusting (*see* trusting stage, of uncertainty)
    welcome talk   92
tracing stage, of uncertainty   92–7
    attempts to trace   94
    attention   94
    'capturing' uncertainty   92
    changing experience of uncertainty   95
    creative practices   93
    open-ended meaning-making   97
    productive ambiguity   97
    re-engaging   93
    re-viewing of video   94
    surrendering   96
    technology   93
    through audio   96
    video recording   92
    volunteers' reflections   94
trusting stage, of uncertainty   99–100
    affirmative design   100
    commitment   100
    confidence   101
    Design+Ethnography+Futures workshops   100
    embracing uncertainty   100
    future-making   100
    sense of optimism   101

Un/certainty ebook   71, 129
Un/certainty symposium   17, 70, 129–30
    frustration and enjoyment   72
    lunch-making activity   72–3
uncertainty
    as acknowledgement   4
    attending to   9
    in contemporary world   1
    creative writing   7

disruptive potential of   59
    (*see also* disruption strategies)
experience of technologies   59–60
generative technology   81
intervention   16
possibility   16
technology of   17–18
uncertainty as concept   19–23
    contemporary obsession   21
    decentring risk   23
    deconstruction of tradition   21
    forms of uncertainty   21
    insistence   23
    institutions of modernity   22
    notion of risk   22
    reflexive individual   21
uncertainty as field of empirical
        study   23–30
    anthropological attention   29
    change-making processes   30
    chaos theory   24
    climate science   24
    competitive gambling   28
    creative uncertainty   27
    disciplinary prioritization   30
    enterprise uncertainty   28
    general force   26
    illusionary mitigation of
        uncertainty   23
    models of jazz improvisation   27
    neoliberal process   25
    notion of resilience   25
    paradigmatic shift   27
    political mediations   25
    possibility of personal gain   29
    problematization approach   26
    risk-averse institutional
        strategies   26–7
    subjective readiness   29
    technologies   26
uncertainty as technology
    change-making   42–3
    disruption (*see* disruption, uncertainty
        as technology for)

generative technology   43
of imagination, experience and action
    (*see* action, uncertainty as
    technology of; experience,
    uncertainty as technology of;
    imagination, uncertainty as
    technology of)
material making   40
messiness of research making   40
messiness of research   42
moving beyond (*see* moving beyond,
        uncertainty as technology for)
objects of analysis   40
re-figuring (*see* re-figuring, uncertainty
        as technology for)
rethinking of things   40
surrender (*see* surrender, uncertainty as
        technology for)
theoretical-methodological
        approach   40
uncertainty postcards   41
uncertainty in research   33–6
    academic audit culture   33
    anthropological mode of uncertainty   34
    co-designing   35
    ethical approval procedures   33
    improvisation   35
    process of design   36
    researcher safety protocols   33
uncertainty postcards   41
understanding uncertainty
    Design+Ethnography+Futures
        symposium   41
    theoretical-methodological approach   40
    uncertainty postcards   41

video ethnography techniques   7–9, 69,
        108, 130
visual documentation   118
visual ethnography   129

'what if'   12, 15, 16, 20
workshops, as form of praxis   12
world-making   3